D0397779

SCOUNDREL TIME

By Lillian Hellman

PLAYS

THE CHILDREN'S HOUR (1934)

DAYS TO COME (1936)

THE LITTLE FOXES (1939)

WATCH ON THE RHINE (1941)

THE SEARCHING WIND (1944)

ANOTHER PART OF THE FOREST (1947)

MONTSERRAT (*An adaptation*, 1950)

THE AUTUMN GARDEN (1951)

THE LARK (*An adaptation*, 1956)

CANDIDE (*An operetta*, 1957)

TOYS IN THE ATTIC (1960)

MY MOTHER, MY FATHER AND ME (*An adaptation*, 1963)

THE COLLECTED PLAYS (1972)

MEMOIRS

AN UNFINISHED WOMAN (1969)

PENTIMENTO (1973)

SCOUNDREL TIME (1976)

EDITOR OF

THE SELECTED LETTERS OF ANTON CHEKHOV (1955)

THE BIG KNOCKOVER: STORIES AND SHORT NOVELS
BY DASHIELL HAMMETT (1966)

SCOUNDREL TIME

by Lillian Hellman

Introduction by Garry Wills

LITTLE, BROWN AND COMPANY · BOSTON · TORONTO

 with photographs

COPYRIGHT © 1976 BY LILLIAN HELLMAN,

INTRODUCTION COPYRIGHT © 1976 BY GARRY WILLS.
ALL RIGHTS RESERVED. NO PART OF THIS BOOK MAY BE REPRODUCED
IN ANY FORM OR BY ANY ELECTRONIC OR MECHANICAL MEANS IN-
CLUDING INFORMATION STORAGE AND RETRIEVAL SYSTEMS WITHOUT
PERMISSION IN WRITING FROM THE PUBLISHER, EXCEPT BY A REVIEWER
WHO MAY QUOTE BRIEF PASSAGES IN A REVIEW.

SECOND PRINTING

T 04/76

LIBRARY OF CONGRESS CATALOGING IN PUBLICATION DATA
Hellman, Lillian, 1905–
  Scoundrel time.

  1. Hellman, Lillian, 1905–   —Biography.
I. Title.
PS3515.E343Z499   812'.5'2 [B]   76-220
ISBN 0-316-35515-1

Published simultaneously in Canada
by Little, Brown & Company (Canada) Limited

PRINTED IN THE UNITED STATES OF AMERICA

For
Barbara and John
Ruth and Marshall
with gratitude for then and now

Introduction

IN 1952 PLAYWRIGHT Lillian Hellman was summoned to testify on her putatively un-American activities before the congressional committee charged with maintaining our Americanism. That was the year when Joseph McCarthy, at the top of his power, was re-elected to the Senate; but she did not appear before his Senate committee. She was summoned by a committee of the lower house — the one which, by its power and long life, became *the* committee of the Cold War period: the House Committee on Un-American Activities (HUAC). For roughly a third of this century the Committee brooded over its ever-growing files, testimony, and reports. Its time of greatest power began in 1948, with its "breaking" of the Hiss case. But as early as 1947 it had declared its wide mandate by posing ideological tests for American artifacts, beginning with the movies.

One movie, made in 1944, especially disturbed Committee members. They called for expert testimony on the film from novelist Ayn Rand, and she quickly identified the work's major flaw: it showed Russians smiling. "It is one of the stock propaganda tricks of the Communists, to show these people smiling." Since Russian propaganda shows Russians smiling, and this American film showed Russians smiling, this American film was part of the Russians' propaganda

3

effort. It is the kind of logic for which Miss Rand is famous, and it dazzled the congressional students who had summoned her in 1947 to instruct them. Richard Nixon was one of her pupils that day, and he had no questions to ask about her Syllogism of the Smiles. Only Representative John McDowell had some reservations:

> McDOWELL: Doesn't anybody smile in Russia anymore?
> RAND: Well, if you ask me literally, pretty much no.
> McDOWELL: They don't smile?
> RAND: Not quite that way, no. If they do, it is privately and accidentally. Certainly, it is not social. They don't smile in approval of their system.

Miss Rand, a screenwriter, must have put some odd directions in her scripts — like: "Smile accidentally, not socially."

Robert Taylor played the lead in *Song of Russia*. Ayn Rand could not forgive him for telling a Russian farmer, "That is wonderful grain." Perhaps Mr. Nixon was making notes during her testimony. Twenty-five years later he would tell the Chinese leaders that their Great Wall is a wonderful wall. (By that time, Russians were telling *us* how nice our grain is.) But Robert Taylor did not have a quarter of a century in which to change his "line" on the Russians. Just three years after he made the movie, and two days after Miss Rand condemned it, he was subpoenaed to meet the charge of trafficking in Russian smiles. He was properly contrite:

4

[COMMITTEE COUNSEL] ROBERT STRIPLING: Mr. Taylor, have you ever participated in any picture as an actor which you considered contained Communist propaganda?

TAYLOR: I assume we are now referring to *Song of Russia.* I must confess that I objected strenuously to doing *Song of Russia* at the time it was made. I felt that it, to my way of thinking, at least, did contain Communist propaganda . . . I don't think it should have been made. I don't think it would be made today.

Why, if he recognized the Communist propaganda, did Mr. Taylor make the movie? Because the chief of movie propaganda in the federal government's Office of War Information had asked him to — we were portraying a brave ally, smiling along with us in the war on Hitler. So why, if he was responding to his own government's request, *recant?* Because one is supposed to anticipate changes in the government's line, agree with the new and reject the old, grateful for the opportunity to repent:

RICHARD NIXON: As far as you are concerned, even though it might mean that you would suffer, possibly, at the box office, possibly in reputation or in other ways, for you to appear before this Committee, you feel you are justified in making the appearance and you would do so again if requested to do so?

TAYLOR: I certainly would, sir. I happen to believe strongly enough in the American people and in what the American people believe in to think that they will go along with anybody who prefers America and the American form of government over any other subversive ideologies which might be preserved and by whom I might be criticized.

This answer got, and deserved, loud applause — anyone who can work America or American four times into a single sentence deserves our admiration.

It was a humiliating little crawl men were learning, that early after World War II. Mr. Taylor even brought names — he had *heard* that the following people might be Communists: Howard Da Silva, Karen Morley, Lester Cole. That put them among those he would, personally, blacklist:

STRIPLING: You would refuse to act in a picture in which a person whom you considered to be a Communist was also cast, is that correct?

TAYLOR: I most assuredly would, and I would not even have to know that he was a Communist. This may sound biased. However, if I were suspicious of a person being a Communist with whom I was scheduled to work, I am afraid it would have to be him or me, because life is a little too short to be around people who annoy me as much as these fellow travelers and Communists do.

Mr. Taylor was now so sensitized to hints from his government that he abruptly changed "line" in the very course of his testimony. Recanting his part in *Song of Russia,* he was led first to this position:

STRIPLING: Mr. Taylor, do you consider that the motion picture primarily is a vehicle of entertainment and not of propaganda?

TAYLOR: I certainly do. I think it is the primary job of

the motion picture industry to entertain; nothing more, nothing less.

STRIPLING: Do you think the industry would be in a better position if it stuck strictly to entertainment without permitting political films to be made?

TAYLOR: I certainly do . . . Every once in a while things do sneak in that nobody catches. If the Communists are not working in the picture business there is no motive for their sneaking things in.

But then the chairman threw out new hints, and Mr. Taylor maneuvered around the full 180 degrees in a mere two sentences:

J. PARNELL THOMAS: Mr. Taylor, are you in favor of the motion picture industry making anti-Communist pictures, giving the facts about Communism?

TAYLOR: Congressman Thomas, when the time arrives — and it might not be long — when pictures of that type are indicated as necessary, I believe the motion picture industry will and should make anti-Communist pictures. When that time is going to be I don't happen to know, but I believe they would and will be made.

The true Party member is ready to denounce his own past at the drop of a hat; but Mr. Taylor set some kind of record in his brief appearance before the Committee, and the Committee succeeded in reducing America to a party and Americanism to its "line." The Committee had already perfected its technique of preemptive ideologizing — the attempt to thwart an enemy by strenuously imitating him.

Of course, the Committee still criticized Communists when *they* exacted ideological conformity and swift conversions. It heard several times how screenwriter Albert Maltz had been disciplined for saying, in a 1946 *New Masses* article, that "writers must be judged by their work and not by the committees they join." Mocking political standards of criticism, he recalled how Lillian Hellman's anti-Nazi play, *Watch on the Rhine,* was denounced by *New Masses* during the time of the Hitler-Stalin pact, and then praised after Hitler's invasion of Russia.

Maltz was called to account for his deviations — typically, at a cell meeting in a Hollywood nightclub. He did his Robert Taylor recanting act in the *Daily Worker.* John Howard Lawson, convener of Marxist salons in Hollywood, was as devout a front-watcher as the Committee's own J. B. Matthews (whose whole first fame rested on the number of fronts *he* had joined).

By 1947 the House Committee on Un-American Activities had been in existence for almost a decade. But it had been a shabby and backstreet operation, specializing in anti-Semitic and racial insinuations under two Southern Democrats as chairmen (Martin Dies and John S. Wood). Respectable Congressmen avoided it. When the nation's best-known anti-Semite, Gerald L. K. Smith, was asked before the Committee in 1946, Representative John Rankin wanted to get his opinion on the evils of the New Deal, not to question him on his anti-Semitic activities. Smith was treated like a friendly expert witness.

But things began to change in 1947. The off-year election of the preceding year had created the first Republican Congress in sixteen years and it seemed to presage the defeat of Harry Truman in 1948. A Republican chairman (J. Parnell Thomas) and chief counsel (Robert Stripling) led the Committee now, and a bright new Congressman like Richard Nixon could see that anxiety over Communism made the Committee a place of opportunity instead of ignominy. A newly aggressive Truman had launched the Cold War in the spring of 1947 with his plan to "rescue" Greece and Turkey. Simultaneously he introduced a new loyalty program, extending investigation to all federal employees (a standard not even imposed in wartime). Truman's Justice Department convened the New York grand jury that would lead to Smith Act prosecutions for mere membership in the Communist Party. The Attorney General arrested Gerhart Eisler under the kind of presidential warrant used in war, and detained him on Ellis Island. J. Edgar Hoover made two personal appearances before the House Committee to call the Communists a "fifth column" justifying the expanded spywork his force had engaged in during the war. Another House committee (Appropriations) launched an attack on ten State Department employees as loyalty risks — and Secretary George Marshall dismissed them all without a hearing. The Senate showed its muscle by getting John Carter Vincent transferred from the Far East desk at State.

But perhaps the most ominous thing that happened in that busy spring of 1947 was the compilation of the Attorney General's List. This was originally proposed as an internal document, to assist in implementing Truman's loyalty tests. A checklist of organizations with four kinds of ties — to Communist, Fascist, totalitarian, or subversive views — would be used to screen federal employees. Membership in one of them, or enough of them, would indicate an area for investigation before an applicant could be approved for a job. Yet later in the year, when Truman was using Attorney General Tom Clark to promote the Marshall Plan as a shield against Communism, the List was published.

This was a profound violation of civil rights in itself, and the basis for all kinds of later violations — by Congress, by individual employers, by entrepreneurial blacklisters. Without charging any illegal acts, without supplying the grounds for its proscription, without offering a machinery for individual reply, the government branded as putatively disloyal any citizen who belonged to one of a large number of organizations. This was soon extended in the public mind to include those who might have given money to one such organization, or attended its meetings. The List, intended to supply prima facie reason for investigating federal employees, was used to deny people employment in *any* responsible position, private or public. The government had made a massive vague charge which it need not sustain in court. And now any private citizen, armed with the List, could impugn another citizen's loyalty with what looked like the authorization of the United States Government. From this single act arose the whole blacklisting campaign, the doctrine of guilt by association, the decade-long search of old letterheads and donations and attendance lists, the cobwebby stringing of "ties" from shadow to shadow.

The McCarthy era does not date from 1950, when Joseph McCarthy made his first charges. It dates from 1947, from the joint efforts of Truman, Attorney General Tom Clark, and J. Edgar Hoover. They gave the House Un-American Activities Committee its weapons — the lists it could use on witnesses, the loyalty program for which it could demand ever stricter enforcement, the presumption that a citizen is disloyal until proved loyal, the denial of work to any man or woman who would not undergo such a proving process. The List meant that everyone must henceforth watch his or her contacts, where one went, whom one saw — a gregarious misstep into the wrong meeting, a check signed for some charitable cause, a more than casual acquaintance with radicals, could put you on the List and forbid you a job. The Attorney General's List was the "original sin" of

McCarthyism. Truman bit into the apple and then, like Adam, cried out indignantly when Cain arrived to slay. Senator Arthur Vandenberg had told Truman he must "scare hell out of the country" if he meant to get his massive foreign program through the Congress. And that is what Truman did.

What made the machinery turn so readily in 1947, launching our vast effort at institutional suspicion and self-policing? We can leave out, here, the mere xenophobes and semiparanoids — understandable types, and so no problem. But what made so many liberal Democrats support the general position of the President and the Attorney General — and even, at the outset, the position of the Committee? We get part of an answer from that exchange between Robert Taylor and Chairman Thomas, in which it is assumed that a Hollywood ready to serve Washington in wartime by making anti-Fascist movies should be just as ready, in 1947, to make anti-Communist (i.e., anti-Russian) movies. There were three equations hidden in that suggestion (a suggestion often repeated in the first Hollywood hearings, with Congressman Nixon especially interested in films directed at Russia). There was, first, an equation of peacetime with a war mobilization of national propaganda. Then there was an equation of Russia, as a national enemy, with "the Axis" of World War II. And finally there was an equation of Russia with Communism — as there had been an equation of Germany, Italy, and even Japan with Fascism in the World War. A nation at war with *ideas* must use ideas as weapons — and the federal government has charge of the national arsenal. Hollywood must be censored politically if the nation was to be protected ideologically.

A nation only partly demobilized by 1947 was very happily, and at once, remobilized. Why? Because of an external threat? Partly, to be sure. But Russia, heavily crippled by the war, still lacking nuclear weaponry, was not a credible threat to our existence then — surely not the kind of threat that would justify so extensive a program of self-defense. Russia's military power did not justify the emergency measures of 1947, including a loyalty program that exceeded even wartime stringencies. Russia was an ideological threat, not a military one; a threat to "Americanism" more than to America — and opposition was made more total because the threat was more subtle. Still, the model for total war was the crusade against Fascism, which was recast as a propaganda ("cold") war of threat and suspicion against Communism.

America in the early 1940's fell in love with total war; and no wonder. The war was the best thing that had happened to this country in a long time. It did what the New Deal never really accomplished — carried us fully out of the Great Depression, and restored us to the boom-expansiveness of our Gilded

Age. It did this by renegotiating the close relationship between business and the federal government — and in the process it expanded the federal government much farther and faster than the New Deal ever did. The nation stretched and rearranged itself — blacks moved North to new jobs, women went into the work market, laboratories and universities and factories expanded with federal money and war programs. By virtue of our brains and effort, we made ourselves the most formidable industrial and military power in the history of the world. Even the secret of the universe's own structure — the atom — served our national goals, which were mankind's and the world's goals.

Americans need to find morality at work behind material success. Money is justified on Horatio Alger grounds, as the reward of virtue and effort. We never doubted our right to use absolute instruments of destruction in World War II — artificially created fire storms, saturation bombing, napalm flamethrowers, both our atom bombs — to enforce our demand for unconditional surrender. Our victory *must* be total, because we were fighting total evil. Winston Churchill piously rumbled that the Germans "must bleed and burn, they must be crushed into a mass of smoldering ruins" — and, of the Japanese, that "we shall wipe them out, every one of them, men, women and children."

We achieved that most refined of pleasures, a

virtuous hate. Killing for an idea is the worst kind of killing, ideological killing. Better to hate a person, the assailant of one's family or home, than to hate an idea. What if the idea hides behind an otherwise law-abiding and unmenacing exterior? Then one must steel oneself against all normal amenities and personal attraction. Then one launches a crusade — to be followed by an inquisition.

It is hard to climb back down from a self-righteous "high" of hatred. The arrogance of victory has been a commonplace at least since Aeschylus's time. And our hate had been given the stunning late justification of Buchenwald and Belsen, the stunning last paroxysms of Hiroshima and Nagasaki. Who could doubt that ours was the purest and most complete victory ever? If power corrupts, we came closer to absolute power, over the world and over our own people's outlook, than any other nation had ever come. Why did we expect to pay no price for this? But when we set about ruling the world we had saved, liberals like Henry Steele Commager chided those who felt there could be anything impure about America's use of its power. He wrote, at the peak of the Cold War: "The record is perhaps unique in the history of power: the organization of the United Nations, the Truman Doctrine, the Marshall Plan, the Berlin airlift, the organization of NATO, the defense of Korea, the development of atomic power for peaceful purposes, Point Four — these prodigious gestures are so wise and so enlightened that they point the way to a new concept of the use of power." Now power purified — and the saints are free of many restrictions imposed on those without proper doctrine.

An essential ingredient of our wartime euphoria had been the concentration of our energies upon a total enemy. In 1946 there was a reluctance to surrender that focusing device. Return to peacetime was looked at warily — wartime had become "normal," preferable to the prewar drift and sluggishness. So we maintained the draft, while Truman fought very hard to impose universal military training on all young males. The OSS was loath to go out of existence. The FBI, expanded to new kinds of power against espionage at home and throughout South America, did not want to give up its new powers. Atomic research continued at full speed and in secret, keeping the issue of security checks alive into peacetime. Crusaders slow to take their armor off get itchy under it, and start to look ridiculous. What could put the moral shine back on that armor but the discovery, off on the horizon, of another Total Enemy? The reluctance of our demobilization in late 1945 explains the rush of glee at our remobilization in early 1947. The liberal second lieutenants and intelligence officers were back in business, and business looked liberal again. We had a world still to save, with just those plans — from NATO to the Korean War — that Professor Commager called "so wise and so enlightened." A thousand wartime ties, relaxed slightly in 1946 to moans of economic and psychic discontent, twanged back tight again and gave America its tonic.

Ideology played its part — give the Red-baiters their due: America has never loved socialism. So did economic interest — give Coolidge his due: America's business never gets far away from Business. But so did psychology — give Aeschylus his due: wars take their toll, especially total wars, and especially a total war against a doctrine won by history's greatest military-scientific breakthrough. As Miss Hellman points out, Americans feared "Bolshies" from 1917 on, but they did not have the instruments for a large-scale investigation or purge. The notorious Palmer Raids had to rely on a small force of federal marshals and an uncooperative Labor Department. But after World War II we had a bloated and ideologized FBI, the congressional committees, an internal security program, a worldwide intelligence operation, and the will to make our Truth prevail. Our postwar world began, instead of ending, with a bang, and we did not intend to whimper. Instead, we bullied.

Bullied, for a start, our own citizenry. But that is part of any crusade. Eleventh-century crusaders first "cleaned out" European ghettos, before getting to the Holy Land. We began World War I by throwing men like Karl Muck into detention, and World War II by imprisoning the Nisei. In 1947 we began what

James Burnham wanted to call World War III by throwing Gerhart Eisler, a German Communist visitor to this country, into a detention camp at Ellis Island. In 1947, by proclamation of the President, we were back at war, and even liberals had long been telling Americans that war obliges them to hate the alien doctrine. We obliged. Communism became exactly what Fascism had been. Our propaganda effort had to be turned against the second enemy just as it had been against the first — Congressman Nixon must "encourage" Hollywood to make anti-Russia movies.

One reason the World War enmities could be so quickly revived, with a new focus on Russia, was the depth of America's understanding of herself as always at odds with alien doctrine. We boast that the nation was brought into being by dedication to a *proposition*, in Lincoln's phrase. We date the country's inception not from the actual inauguration of constitutional government but from the declaration of our principles thirteen years earlier. An element in America's sense of mission has always been the belief that close foreign ties might sully the purity of republican doctrine, a fear expressed by Jefferson himself. It was not enough to be American in citizenship or residence — one must be American in one's thoughts. There was such a thing as Americanism. And lack of right thinking could make an American citizen un-American. The test was ideological. That is why we had such a thing as an Un-American Activities Committee in the first place. Other countries do not think in terms of, say, Un-British Activities as a political category. But ours was the first of the modern ideological countries, born of revolutionary doctrine, and it has maintained a belief that return to doctrinal purity is the secret of national strength for us.

It is typical that the very term "un-American activities" was first advanced by a liberal, Representative Samuel Dickstein, who proposed in 1934 that a permanent committee be established to look into the pro-German sympathies of the German-American Bund. It is also typical that in 1938, when the Committee was finally brought into being, it was the result of a compromise with those who wanted to investigate radicals and socialists as well as Fascists. Liberals in America have often elaborated an ideological test which the right wing applies more broadly and ferociously than the liberals originally intended. That is the story of Truman's loyalty program and purge of the State Department in 1947. These moves are sometimes made with a hope that they will obviate more repressive acts by the right; but instead they legitimate the later, harsher measures. All later excesses arise from the first principle of ideological self-testing. If it is not enough to possess citizenship and obey the laws, if one must also subscribe to the propositions of Americanism, then we create two classes of citizens — those loyal and pure in doctrine, and those who, without actually breaking any law, are considered un-American, insufficient in their Americanism. These latter can be harassed, spied on, forced to register, deprived of governmental jobs and other kinds of work.

It is easy to explain in this way the FBI's harassment, going far beyond enforcement of the law, of the Ku Klux Klan. After all, our country was conceived in liberty and dedicated to the proposition that all men are created equal. Since the Klan did not believe in the proposition, it was not fully American, even when it was not breaking the law. But once you set up such a division within the citizenry, you open a Pandora's box. How are we to know what others think about the doctrines of Americanism unless we investigate their thoughts, make them profess their loyalty, train children up in the government's orthodoxy? Aren't we always at war with error, both at home and abroad — and aren't wartime measures always justifiable? Aren't we all insufficiently dedicated to our self-constituting doctrine, and so must test ourselves, make demands on ourselves, train ourselves to fuller Americanism? We are not merely a country. We are an Ism. And truth must spread without limit; it cannot countenance error. So John F. Kennedy orated: "In the election of 1860 Abraham Lincoln said the question was whether this nation could exist half-slave or half-free. In the election of 1960, and with the world around us, the question is whether the world will exist half-slave or half-free." In the war of minds, anyone not fully committed to the propositions of freedom is an enemy. The reign of the Committee had long historical forces to draw on, explaining its power.

It is unfortunate that McCarthyism was named teleologically, from its most perfect product, rather than genetically — which would give us Trumanism. By studying "McCarthyism" in terms of Joseph McCarthy's own period of Red-baiting (1950–1954), a number of scholars have called the disease an imbalance between Congress and the Executive (thus contributing to a pre-Nixon glorification of the imperial presidency). It is true that the Executive opposed investigative committees by McCarthy's time; but in 1947 the President not only cooperated with these committees, but gave them the means to grow powerful. Secretary of State George Marshall cooperated with Senator Styles Bridges and Congressman John Taber in purging the State Department. Attorney General Clark cooperated with the House Committee in its Eisler "investigation." J. Edgar Hoover appeared before the Committee to praise its work and get congressional support for his own vast loyalty probings. In March of 1947, when Truman issued his executive order for loyalty tests, he designated HUAC files as an official source of evidence on employees' ties. The Committee congratulated him for his action, and took credit for purging the Executive. The Hollywood hearings of 1947 did not threaten Truman — the farther the Committee looked from Washington, the happier he was. Only when the Committee tried to steal the spotlight from the Justice Department's own work before the grand jury in New York did Truman ease up on his cooperation with the Committee — and by then it was too late. The grand jury had heard a witness named Whittaker Chambers, and Congressman Nixon had received from that witness some documents he would not yield to the grand jury.

Yet even when Truman dismissed the Committee's hearings as a "red herring" in the fall of 1948, he was not taking the hard stand that he would in McCarthy's time. He meant that conducting any investigative work in this special session of Congress, which he had demanded between the conventions and the election, was a distraction from the job of passing his economic program. Actually, the Committee's 1948 triumph in the Hiss case had worked to Truman's advantage. Alger Hiss may have been associated with the New Deal in the past, but his present work was with John Foster Dulles at the Carnegie Endowment for International Peace. More important, the principal witness against Hiss, Whittaker Chambers, claimed a Communist group had been formed within Henry Wallace's New Deal Agricultural Adjustment Administration; and two of those named — Lee Pressman and John Abt — were working prominently in Wallace's 1948 presidential campaign. Two more of Wallace's supporters — Harry Dexter White and Victor Perlo — were called Communists by Committee witness Elizabeth Bentley. The Committee actually summoned these people to testify during the campaign — they pleaded the Fifth Amendment. Truman had feared the Wallace threat more than a Southern split, and his workers took elaborate steps to contain that threat. The Committee completed their work.

Henry Wallace had broken with the Truman administration on the aggressive new turn our foreign policy had taken by 1947. He saw the NATO alliance, in particular, as a de facto substitute for all our commitments to the United Nations, a confession that peace had given way to war. His analysis of the Dean Acheson strategy, moving from the Truman Doctrine to the Marshall Plan to the Atlantic alliance, resembles that made by today's revisionist historians — and proves that their analysis is not something available only to hindsight. What is more, the effectiveness of Wallace's first criticism proves that the Acheson world vision only later acquired its air of unquestionable rectitude. The administration was busy draping flags all over these programs in 1947 — but it feared some flags would slip. When Wallace first broke with Truman, a poll showed 24 percent of Democrats willing to vote for him against Truman. There was still some question whether Truman was a proper heir to the New Deal. But Wallace, who was Roosevelt's first wartime Vice-President, had also been one of the original New Dealers.

Clark Clifford, Truman's campaign strategist, identified Wallace as the principal threat to re-election in his famous memo of November 1947. He said Truman should head off this threat by "some top-level appointments from the ranks of the progressives," by offering a civil rights program ("the South can be . . . safely ignored"), and by "isolating" Wallace: "The Administration must persuade prominent liberals and progressives — and no one else — to move publicly into the fray. They must point out that the core of Wallace's backing is made up of Communists and fellow travelers." It would be the job of prominent liberals — which meant, principally, of Americans for Democratic Action — to do the Committee's kind of work in a more sophisticated way, and to do it on their fellows.

The ADA was ready. America's "best and brightest" had conducted America's triumphant crusade against Fascism as officers, scientists, foreign experts, intelligence men. They meant to continue America's benevolent disposal of the world's freedoms, using the tools of their mind (especially the bomb) to enforce their Wilsonian vision of the world. If they had to win support in a still isolationist country by a little saber-rattling ("scare hell out of the country"), the gains were worth the price. Besides, it was easy

for any liberal to have been at meetings now stig-
matized by the Attorney General's List, or to have
worked closely with Russians during the war. Show
business witnesses before the Committee learned what
columnists to go to for reinstatement as a loyal American — Hedda Hopper on the West Coast, George
Sokolsky on the East Coast. By 1947 the liberal intellectual's way to establish his anti-Communist cre-
dentials was through the ADA, developed on the base
of Reinhold Niebuhr's "pragmatic" wartime Union
for Democratic Action. Formed in the wake of the
1946 election, which gave Congress to the Republi-
cans, the ADA thought it could prevent further reaction by carrying on its own purge of Communists.
When the Marshall Plan was proposed, such liberals
made it the touchstone of enlightened anti-Communism. The ADA accepted the heritage of the New
Deal along with that of the OSS. (The CIA was another of Truman's gifts to us in 1947.)

Critics of Truman's aggressiveness formed, in
1947, the Progressive Citizens of America, which was
a kind of anti-ADA in several senses, including an
unwillingness to undertake its own purges just because
the government might purge them less discrimina-
tingly later on. They naïvely thought that purges were
not the business of American political organizations.
The few serious Communists left in open political
life belonged to the PCA. So did radicals like Lillian
Hellman. When Henry Wallace looked around for

support in his 1948 campaign, most of the intellectual
support came from the PCA, and Miss Hellman cam-
paigned for him full-time.

Miss Hellman is not only the leading woman
playwright of our time, but of our nation's entire
history. Her stage works were not crudely political,
like the products of the Workers' Theater — which
may explain why she missed the first go-round of
Hollywood investigations. (She had been one of the
more successful screenwriters.) She was certainly
not passed over for any unwillingness, on her part, to
join in radical causes. Her list must have warmed
the heart of J. B. Matthews on cold nights. Besides,
she had lived for decades with Dashiell Hammett, who
was probably a Communist. Miss Hellman's prom-
inence in the Wallace campaign no doubt put her on
several hundred more lists. But she really drew the
Communist-hunters' eye by her sponsorship of the
Cultural and Scientific Conference for World Peace
held at the Waldorf-Astoria Hotel in the spring of
1949.

The Waldorf Conference is largely forgotten now,
but it tied up most of the State Department at the
time. Talmudic decisions were announced on who
would get visas from each country, and who wouldn't.
The department issued a twenty-six-page white paper
on the eve of the conference explaining that it had
not let some artists and scholars enter the country because *Russia* is even *worse* about allowing free entry

, to the loss of one's job. The at-
or status, or an Academy Award,
y Parks and Elia Kazan and Jose
e guiltless in order to sweeten their
into what the Committee would call
awl was more abject than in Robert
sold you and you sold me."
remember the period in order to un-
act of Lillian Hellman's 1952 letter
ee: "I cannot and will not cut my
t this year's fashions." Because she
mmittee that she would take the Fifth
name others, she was confessedly not
erly" — that is, in her own defense.
been held in contempt, and some were
she was not. *Time* magazine implied
off by theatrics — her lawyer, Joseph
uted copies of her statement at her

agement was especially dangerous be-
Hellman was as little qualified to un-
Committee as it was to grasp her
or. She writes that she cannot believe
Carthy and Chambers were sincere. The
mentality is so foreign to her that she
fanaticism to herself as mere opportun-
ct, the Red-hunters were so dangerous
ecause they considered themselves saviors
try from a diabolical plot.

(again, the preemptive ideologizing). The sessions were prowled by a concentration of intelligence services unheard of then but commonplace now. At the final session, police allowed one thousand pickets to circulate, but had to turn away five thousand more. The intellectual community was divided. Sidney Hook formed a counter-conference for anti-Communist intellectuals, sponsored by the ad hoc Americans for Intellectual Freedom. Men like Arthur Schlesinger, Jr., and James Wechsler rallied to Hook's call. Other guardians of American liberalism, like Mary McCarthy and Dwight Macdonald, went to sessions of the conference in order to disrupt them. Dimitri Shostakovich was, in the name of freedom, publicly insulted for not being free. Norman Cousins, who had refused to attend the opening session of the conference, changed his mind when the State Department asked him to go and attack the conference, telling the foreign guests that their hosts were a small and dishonored part of America. This caused an uproar, which dissolved into laughter when Miss Hellman said, at the podium: "I didn't know until now that one talked about one's host at his dinner table. I recommend my own method, Mr. Cousins, which is to wait until you get home to do it."

Miss Hellman had herself been asked by our own government's authorities to visit Russia during World War II — before we changed *that* line. She formed friendships there not subject to any government's line, so she helped arrange for artists and scholars to meet and discuss what would later (when a new line came in) be called "detente." It was a difficult thing to propose, and even harder to accomplish. The government tried to prevent the meeting by using its weird visa rules. In the end, admitted Communists had a better chance to attend than mere leftists from abroad — the Communist countries got their spokesmen visas as official representatives of their country (they would be attacked, while here, for representing their country — if they had *not* been representatives, we would not have given them entry). The four participants from England, none of them Communists, were denied visas. So was a Catholic priest from France. Patriotic organizations reminded America that we must keep ourselves free — free of exposure to such people.

By now the House Committee was clearly being remiss in not calling Miss Hellman. The fear and hatred of Communists hardened in 1949, with Mao's conquest of China, Russia's explosion of an atomic bomb, and in June 1950 with the beginning of the Korean War. In 1950 McCarthy made his first charges and Alger Hiss was convicted. The scene was set for the onslaught of McCarthyism proper. In March of 1951 the Rosenbergs were condemned to death, and the Committee began a new round of Hollywood hearings. In June, Dashiell Hammett refused to name contributors to a Civil Rights Congress bail fund, and

it
ci
the
195
wou
Ever
drew
Comm
nist-h
Rosenl
had be
ting sho
anymore
other fue
framewor
eral Mars
was disloy
fed suspici
ering up, th
witnesses su
was more sev
Fifth Amendr
fense in the p
answer of guilt

led, in many case
tempt to save jobs
led men like Lar
Ferrer to name t
own guiltlessness
innocence. The
Taylor's time. "
One has to
derstand the in
to the Commi
conscience to
notified the C
only if forced
taking it "pr
She could ha
surprised th
that she got
Rauh, distr
appearance
The e
cause Miss
derstand
code of
men like
ideologue
must exp
ism. In
precisely
of the co

One of the unfortunate results of our generally muddled political terminology is a tendency to think of those on what is called the left as points on a continuum moving out from the center. The difference between, say, liberals, socialists, radicals, and Communists is a matter of degree within a continuum. (The Committee liked to work with this model, but so — surprisingly — have many people on the left.) But there are basic differences between some of these groups that matter more than any "geographical" location on a leftist spectrum. Cold War liberals were ideologues, and ideologues meet each other on the same ground, if only to do battle there. Radicals of the Hellman and Hammett sort cannot even find that meeting place. The popular image of the radical is of the wild and irresponsible "bomb thrower." But most radicals I have met were extraordinarily civil. They oppose the general degradation, not with a programmatic "solution," but with a personal code that makes pride possible in a shameful social order. They do not wish to be implicated in responsibility for society's crimes, which means that they must take a special kind of responsibility for their own acts.

Ideology is, by contrast, an *escape* from personal responsibility. Someone like Whittaker Chambers wanted to be told what to do, wanted to be History's slave. Ideologues want to be certified by others as respectable — if not by the Committee or the Party, then by the ADA. They want their hates to be dictated by the national program. The radical thinks of virtuous people, while the ideologue thinks of orthodoxy. The radical hates vicious and harmful people, while the ideologue hates heretical ideas, no matter how "nice" the possessors of those ideas may be. The radical tries to uphold a private kind of honor in a rotten world — like Hammett's "private eyes," serving society without respecting it, seeing men and not just abstract Crime in the victims of their hunt. Hammett wielded that most self-wounding of human instruments, irony; and ironists make terrible crusaders. The worst thing one could have wished on the mousy world of Communist ideologues in America was a dozen more Hammetts.

Lillian Hellman grew up in the South, a place of ambivalent moral ferocities, but also of intensest personalism. She is to ideology what Faulkner was to racism — too engaged in personal loves and hates to sort out hatred on a program. Radicals make good haters, since they concentrate their hate. Ideological hatred is colder, but more diffuse — a thing of long lists and long memories, of inclusive impersonal vendettas, of a calm voraciousness. This cold face of ideology is so distant from Miss Hellman's moral world as to be almost invisible. She has spent her life creating vivid and individual people on the stage; the thought of a McCarthy intent on destroying whole classes and types of people is almost too horrible for her to contemplate.

Hilaire Belloc wrote that Danton was destroyed because he obtruded common sense upon a Program. Yet Danton had helped launch the revolutionary program. His relation to Robespierre was that of the Cold War liberals to the Committee. For, oddly enough, the extreme of Cold War liberalism, on a continuum of American thinking, was not a radicalism of the left, but — the Committee itself.

This was not Miss Hellman's battle. She came to it armed with no ideological weapons, just with that personal code, with undefended decency — which is, on occasion, the strongest weapon of all. The extraordinary impact of her appearance comes from this non-ideological appeal straight to personal emotions of pride and loyalty, the kind of "loyalty" that meant nothing to the Committee but made its tests ring silly and false. Joseph Rauh, who went on to defend other witnesses before the Committee, says that Lillian's stand made it much easier for those who followed her to defy that dread request for names. Eric Bentley calls her stand a "landmark" in his book on the Committee, and Walter Goodman notes that Arthur Miller repeated her arguments almost exactly when he appeared. Murray Kempton found her testimony a sign of hope in that darkest farthest reach of McCarthyism.

Despite her literary stature, she seems an unlikely heroine for that grim time, a blend of sassy kid and Southern lady, scared but defiant in her Balmain "testifying dress." But we must remember that Dashiell Hammett modeled Nora Charles after her in *The Thin Man* (which Senator McCarthy tried to have removed from our overseas bookshelves). And when a policeman encounters Nora at her most independent, he leaves shaking his head in reluctant admiration and calling her one tough lady. Chairman Wood probably felt like that on the afternoon of May 21, 1952.

GARRY WILLS

SCOUNDREL TIME

I HAVE TRIED TWICE BEFORE to write about what has come to be known as the McCarthy period but I didn't much like what I wrote. My reasons for not being able to write about my part in this sad, comic, miserable time of our history were simple to me, although some people thought I had avoided it for mysterious reasons. There was no mystery. I had strange hangups and they are always hard to explain. Now I tell myself that if I face them, maybe I can manage.

The prevailing eccentricity was and is my inability to feel much against the leading figures of the period, the men who punished me. Senators McCarthy and McCarran, Representatives Nixon, Walter and Wood, all of them, were what they were: men who invented when necessary, maligned even when it wasn't necessary. I do not think they believed much, if anything, of what they said: the time was ripe for a new wave in America, and they seized their political chance to lead it along each day's opportunity, spitballing whatever and with whoever came into view.

But the new wave was not so new. It began with the Russian Revolution of 1917. The victory of the revolution, and thus its menace, had haunted us through the years that followed, then twisted the tail of history when Russia was our ally in the Second

World War and, just because that had been such an unnatural connection, the fears came back in fuller force after the war when it looked to many people as if Russia would overrun Western Europe. Then the revolution in China caused an enormous convulsion in capitalist societies and somewhere along the line gave us the conviction that we could have prevented it if only. If only was never explained with any sense, but the times had very little need of sense.

The fear of Communism did not begin that year, but the new China, allied in those days with Russia, had a more substantial base and there were many honest men and women who were, understandably, frightened that their pleasant way of life could end in a day.

It was not the first time in history that the confusions of honest people were picked up in space by cheap baddies who, hearing a few bars of popular notes, made them into an opera of public disorder, staged and sung, as much of the congressional testimony shows, in the wards of an insane asylum.

A theme is always necessary, a plain, simple, unadorned theme to confuse the ignorant. The anti-Red theme was easily chosen from the grab bag, not alone because we were frightened of socialism, but chiefly, I think, to destroy the remains of Roosevelt and his sometimes advanced work. The McCarthy group — a loose term for all the boys, lobbyists, Congressmen, State Department bureaucrats, CIA operators —

chose the anti-Red scare with perhaps more cynicism than Hitler picked anti-Semitism. He, history can no longer deny, deeply believed in the impurity of the Jew. But it is impossible to remember the drunken face of McCarthy, merry often with a kind of worldly malice, as if he were mocking those who took him seriously, and believe that he himself could take seriously anything but his boozed-up nightmares. And if all the rumors were true the nightmares could have concerned more than the fear of a Red tank on Pennsylvania Avenue, although it is possible that in his case a tank could have turned him on. Mr. Nixon's beliefs, if indeed they ever existed, are best left to jolly quarter-historians like Theodore White. But one has a right to believe that if Whittaker Chambers * was capable of thinking up a pumpkin, and he was, Mr. Nixon seized upon this strange hiding place with the eagerness of a man who already felt deep contempt for public intelligence. And he was right.

But none of them, even on the bad morning of my hearing before the House Un-American Activities Committee, interested me or disturbed me at a serious

* In August 1948 Whittaker Chambers appeared before the House Un-American Activities Committee. Chambers, a senior editor of *Time* magazine, told the Committee that he had once been a Communist and an underground courier. He named ten men as his former associates, the best known being Alger Hiss, formerly a high official of the State Department. Chambers accused Hiss of giving him secret government material, which Chambers preserved by placing it in a pumpkin at his farm in Maryland. Hiss was indicted, tried twice, and sent to jail for almost four years. In 1975 the secret pumpkin papers were found to contain nothing secret, nothing confidential. They were, in fact, nonclassified, which is Washington's way of saying anybody who says please can have them.

level. They didn't and they don't. They are what they are, or were, and are no relation to me by blood or background. (My own family held more interesting villains of another, wittier nature.)

I have written before that my shock and my anger came against what I thought had been the people of my world, although in many cases, of course, I did not know the men and women of that world except by name. I had, up to the late 1940's, believed that the educated, the intellectual, lived by what they claimed to believe: freedom of thought and speech, the right of each man to his own convictions, a more than implied promise, therefore, of aid to those who might be persecuted. But only a very few raised a finger when McCarthy and the boys appeared. Almost all, either by what they did or did not do, contributed to McCarthyism, running after a bandwagon which hadn't bothered to stop to pick them up.

Simply, then and now, I feel betrayed by the nonsense I had believed. I had no right to think that American intellectuals were people who would fight for anything if doing so would injure them; they have very little history that would lead to that conclusion. Many of them found in the sins of Stalin Communism — and there were plenty of sins and plenty that for a long time I mistakenly denied — the excuse to join those who should have been their hereditary enemies. Perhaps that, in part, was the penalty of nineteenth-century immigration. The children of timid immigrants are often remarkable people: energetic, intelligent, hardworking; and often they make it so good that they are determined to keep it at any cost. The native grandees, of course, were glad to have them as companions on the conservative ship: they wrote better English, had read more books, talked louder and with greater fluency.

But I don't want to write about my historical conclusions — it isn't my game. I tell myself that this third time out, if I stick to what I know, what happened to me, and a few others, I have a chance to write my own history of the time.

I DO NOT KNOW the year when I, who had always been a kind of aimless rebel — not only in the sense that was true of most of my generation, but because I had watched my mother's family increase their fortune on the borrowings of poor Negroes — found that my rebelliousness was putting down a few young political roots. I think that began with the discovery of National Socialism when I was in Bonn, Germany, intending to enroll at the university. It took me months to understand what I was listening to. Then for the first time in my life I thought about being a Jew. But I was not only listening to anti-Semitism. I was hearing from people my own age the boasts of hopeful conquerors, the sounds of war.

I came home to an economic depression that was to break my father, although it treated Arthur Kober, to whom I was married, very well with a job as a scenario writer in Hollywood. But even his good salary meant less than it should have because the storms in the movie industry were so great that the luck of the day was just that and nothing more.

In any case, Arthur's good job didn't matter much to me because I got a divorce in 1931 and couldn't find a job. True, I didn't need one very much because by that time I was living with the writer Dashiell Hammett, who not only earned a great deal but shared it with me, or with anybody else who came along. But that was no answer, either: if you have worked, living on other people's money isn't a solution. For three or four years there was to be no solution for me, although Roosevelt's election gave many people, me among them, our first feelings that maybe we could have something to do with our own futures, through our own government. (Obviously nobody could have anything to do with the governments of Coolidge or Hoover.)

At the end of 1934 my first play, *The Children's Hour,* was a great success. The days of living on other people were over, and it was in many ways a mighty nice time. But success caused a kind of guilt. I am suspicious of guilt in myself and in other people: it is usually a way of not thinking, or of announcing one's own fine sensibilities the better to be rid of them fast. But about this guilt, the guilt that came from my own good luck, I am still pleased because it led somewhere. I am not even displeased with the troubles it was to cause me.

I have written before, and must write again, about Dashiell Hammett because he was so large a part of my life in the Thirties and Forties. (And for much longer, of course, but that is another story.) The middle and late Thirties were a time when many people were turning toward radical political solutions, and he was one of them, with me trailing behind, worried often about what didn't worry him, inhibited by what he ignored. I am fairly sure that Hammett joined the Communist Party in 1937 or 1938. I do not know because I never asked, and if I had asked would not have been answered, and my not asking, knowing there would be no answer, was typical of our relationship. I did not join the Party, although mild overtures were made by Earl Browder and the Party theorist, V. J. Jerome.

I did go, three or four times, with Hammett to meetings: two in an ugly Spanish house in Hollywood; one or two in New York in an apartment I don't remember, with people I don't remember, maybe because I left after a short time. In the Hollywood meetings there were seven or eight people. I knew three of them slightly, but the others were something I then called "unaesthetic." Certainly the fact that what seemed to be the chairman, or leader, had a habit of tying and untying his shoelaces, making strange cut-outs from pieces of yellow pad paper and throwing the cutouts to the floor, took my attention away from what might have been a serious discussion. Another man kept using the phrase "the face of the Party," and since all expert phrases interest me, I wanted very much to find out what that meant. Two ladies, one youngish, one middle-aged, talked a great deal, mostly to each other and always in high irritation. The middle-aged lady, I found out later, owned a fashionable dress shop, and I was impressed with the force of the conviction that had made her join a radical group when any gossip about her affiliations would have cost her a fine business. (I didn't need to worry; when the real Red-baiting days began she moved her shop to Santa Barbara and never again spoke to her brother, who went to jail for his Communist Party affiliations.) Either at the first or second of these Hollywood meetings, the Spanish Civil War was discussed. I was surprised that when I complained the Russians had not sent enough supplies — I had just come home from Spain in the autumn of 1937 — but only enough to keep the Spanish fighting and dying for a cause that was going to be lost, nobody disagreed with me or defended the Soviet Union. Maybe they agreed, maybe they didn't think I was worth arguing with.

Russia: they made use of their anti-Communism to play ball with the wrong people and many of them are still at it.

I am, of course, making my political history too simple: personal conflicts, work problems, whiskey, too much money after *The Children's Hour*, the time of my time, Hammett, all had to do with whatever I believed.

It was true that Hammett became a committed radical and I didn't, but strangely enough when we first met I think it was I, and not he, who had come to certain unshakable conclusions. I remember sitting on a bed next to him in the first months we met, listening to him tell me about his Pinkerton days when an officer of Anaconda Copper Company had offered him five thousand dollars to kill Frank Little, the labor union organizer. I didn't know Hammett well enough to hear the anger under the calm voice, the bitterness under the laughter, so I said, "He couldn't have made such an offer unless you had been strike-breaking for Pinkerton."

"That's about right," he said.

I walked into his living room thinking I don't want to be here, I don't want to be with this man. I went back to the door of the bedroom to tell him that.

He was leaning on his elbow, facing the door, as if he expected me. He said, "Yes, ma'm. Why do you think I told you?"

He seldom talked about the past unless I asked

questions, but through the years he was to repeat that bribe offer so many times that I came to believe, knowing him now, that it was a kind of key to his life. He had given a man the right to think he would murder, and the fact that Frank Little was lynched with three other men in what was known as the Everett Massacre must have been, for Hammett, an abiding horror. I think I can date Hammett's belief that he was living in a corrupt society from Little's murder. In time, he came to the conclusion that nothing less than a revolution could wipe out the corruption. I do not mean to suggest that his radical conversion was based on one experience, but sometimes in complex minds it is the plainest experience that speeds the wheels that have already begun to move.

It is necessary here to repeat what I have written about before. There were perhaps twenty years between my hearing about Frank Little and Hammett's jail sentence in 1951. During those twenty years we did not always live together, did not always share the same house or the same city, and even when we were together we both had unspoken but strict rules about privacy. And so I have no real knowledge of his affiliations to the Communist Party. He went to jail in 1951 for refusing to give the names of the contributors to the bail bond fund of the Civil Rights Congress, of which he was one of the trustees. I don't remember ever hearing the name of the organization until about a month before he was arrested, and that may be because he had never been in their offices. He was sent to the filthy West Street jail in New York, in an unprecedented judgment that allowed no bail, and then moved to the federal prison in Ashland, Kentucky.

He was sickish when he went to jail, and he came out sicker, but he took all of it in fine spirits, obviously pleased with his ability to take whatever punishment had come to him or might come in the future. But his nature was not mine. He had known that if you differ from society, no matter how many pieties they talk they will punish you for disturbing them. No such thing had ever occurred to me; when I disagreed I was exercising my inherited rights, and certainly there could be no punishment for doing what I had been taught to do by teachers, books, American history. It was not only my right, it was my duty to speak or act against what I thought was wrong or dangerous. It is comically late to admit that I did not even consider the fierce, sweeping, violent nonsense-tragedies that break out in America from time to time, one of which was well on its way after World War II.

Hammett's reaction to jail was odd and often irritating: he talked of his time there the way I remembered young men talking about their survival in a severe prep school or a tough football game. He was always pleased that he could adapt to whatever was necessary; he had gone through almost three years of the miseries of the Aleutian-Alaskan weather during the war and several times seriously proposed to me that we move there for good. They were mysterious reactions to me. Now, so many years later, I know they came from plain, old-fashioned self-discipline as it mixed with plain, old-fashioned pride.

In any case, his feelings about jail when I was faced with jail did me no good. I knew that I could not stand what he could stand. I have temper and it is triggered at odd times by odd matters and is then out of my control: if I am kept waiting when I think it is unnecessary, if I am shoved in a bus or subway, finding myself or anybody else treated with disrespect, being unjustly accused of what I didn't do even if the accusation is about something trivial — a whole set of reactions happen which I am unable, at the minute of temper, to recognize as childish. Hammett knew all about me, stuff like that, and so when I was threatened with jail, less than a year after he came out, he used what he knew to try to keep me from what he didn't believe I could safely take. Maybe he was right, maybe he wouldn't have been. I could not know then or now because we did not share what the French call a neurosis for two. We each had our own little bundle, but they did not mix, or cross or rub off on one another. His fears for me began on February 21, 1952.

I OWNED AND LIVED in a lovely neo-Georgian house on East 82nd Street, with one tenant above me. As in most such houses, visitors rang a downstairs bell and then were asked to announce themselves into an instrument. It had never been possible to hear anything but garble from the instrument, so I had grown tired of it and long before had taken to pressing the bell when anyone rang and waiting for the small elevator to rise to my floor. An over-respectable-looking black man, a Sunday deacon, in a suit that was so correct-incorrect that it could be worn only by somebody who didn't want to be noticed, stood in the elevator, his hat politely removed. He asked me if I was Lillian Hellman. I agreed to that and asked who he was. He handed me an envelope and said he was there to serve a subpoena from the House Un-American Activities Committee. I opened the envelope and read the subpoena. I said, "Smart to choose a black man for this job. You like it?" and slammed the door.

I sat with the subpoena for perhaps an hour, alone in the house, not wishing to talk to anybody. There it was, and for some reason there seemed to me nothing to hurry about. I took to looking at the last few days' mail, some of it already dictated for a secretary who came twice a week, some of it yet to be answered. One of the forms I had filled out a few days before, ready for mailing, was the usual questionnaire from *Who's Who in America*. I suppose I found some amusement in reading it again: I had by that day written *The Children's Hour, Days to Come, The Little Foxes, Watch on the Rhine, The Searching Wind, Another Part of the Forest, The Autumn Garden.* I had collected and introduced a volume of Chekhov letters, written movies and tinkered with others, belonged to organizations, unions — all the stuff I always have to look up from the previous *Who's Who* because I can't remember the dates.

Then I took a nap and woke up in a sweat of bewilderment about myself. I telephoned Hammett and he said he would take the next train from Katonah, so to sit still and do nothing until he got there. But the calm was gone now and I couldn't do that.

I went immediately to Stanley Isaacs, who had been borough president of Manhattan and who had suffered under an attack, led by Robert Moses, because one of his minor assistants was a member of the Communist Party. Stanley had stood up well under the attack, although, of course, the episode hurt his very Republican career. (I had gone to him as an admiring stranger as soon as he returned to his own law practice and had brought along with me, in the following years, quite a few people who liked and admired him.) Isaacs was an admirable man, but I think by the time of my subpoena he was more worried than he wanted to admit, and knew that his way back to politics — he was, in fact, never to have a way back — could be mended only with care. Isaacs and I were fond of each other and his face looked pained as he told me that he didn't believe he should handle the case, he didn't know enough about the field, but together we would find the right man.

Together we didn't. Stanley had a number of suggestions during the next few days, but I didn't like any of them, and while I remember that clearly, it is strange that I don't remember how I came, on my own, to phone Abe Fortas. I had never met Fortas, although I had, of course, heard of him and his law firm of Arnold, Fortas and Porter. Mr. Fortas said he was coming to New York the next day and would come by and see me.

But if I don't remember how I came to phone Fortas, I do remember everything about our meeting: the nasty weather outside the tall windows; the thin, intelligent face opposite me in an Empire chair that seemed wrong for him; most of all, the eyes that were taking my measure, a business that has always made me nervous and was making me more nervous on this nervous day. I told him about the subpoena, he asked a few questions about my past, none of any real importance, he admired the china birds on the fireplace, he tried out a few notes on the piano, frowned at the tone, and turned to say that he had a hunch he'd tell me about, but I was not to take a hunch as legal advice.

His hunch was that the time had come, the perfect time, for somebody to take a moral position before these disgraceful congressional committees and not depend on the legalities of the Fifth Amendment. To Fortas the moral position would be to say, in essence, I will testify about myself, answer all your questions about my own life, but I will not tell you about anybody else, stranger or friend. Fortas thought that I might be in a good position to say just that because, in truth, I didn't know much about anybody's Communist affiliations. The Committee would never, of course, believe that, and so my legal rights would be in danger because I would be giving up the protection of the Fifth Amendment. I wanted to tell him that the moral position for my taste would be to say, "You are a bunch of headline seekers, using other people's lives for your own benefits. You know damn well that the people you've been calling before you never did much of anything, but you've browbeaten and bullied many of them into telling lies about sins they never committed. So go to hell and do what you want with me." I didn't say any of that to Fortas because I knew I would never be able to say it at all.

(But for five or six years after my appearance before the Committee, when other troubles came, and I would be sleepless, I would get up at odd hours of the night and write versions of the statement I never made. I was certain that whatever would have been the injuries of jail they could not have been as bad as I had thought in those first days. Then, of course, when I had climbed back into bed to read a new and fancier version of what I hadn't said, I would think it's fine to do all this after the fears are over, you'd better cut it out and start worrying about how you will act when trouble comes again.)

What I did that afternoon of Mr. Fortas's visit was to say that I agreed with him and thought his idea was right for me. But he wouldn't have it that way; he said that I must take a few days and think it out carefully and then call him. I said I didn't need the few days and he said maybe, but he did need them, he wanted to think over what he had suggested. Before Fortas left he said that neither he nor his firm could take my case because they were representing Owen Lattimore and Lattimore could hurt me or I could hurt Lattimore. But he knew a fine young lawyer and we'd talk about him the next time we met.

Mine is often an irritable nature. If the groceries haven't arrived on time, or the corn grows stunted, or the phone rings too much, even with good news, I am, as I have said, sometimes out of control. But when there is real trouble, the nervousness gets pushed down so far that calm takes its place, and although I pay high for disaster when it is long past, I am not sure that real trouble registers on me when it first appears. I don't know why that happens, but I think I have the sense to understand that there is nothing to do but to face trouble with a roped control, and that any suspicion of high jinks will break me. That was where I was for the next few months — more important, for the next bad week.

The day after the visit from Fortas, I told Hammett what I was going to do. Dash rarely showed anger, but when he did, it came out in the form of staring at me. The staring would often go on for a long time, as if he were thinking over how you dealt with a crazy lady, what was the best way out. I had been through the stare periods many times in the past, but now it went longer than I could stand and I grew uneasy enough to go for a walk. When I came back we spoke of nothing more than what we would cook for dinner and I made the mistake of thinking that he had decided to say nothing, to mind his own business, which was what he usually did after the anger had passed. But I was wrong: halfway through dinner he pushed his plate away and said, "It's shit. Plain liberal shit. They are going to send you to a jail cell and for longer than usual. I don't give a damn what Mr. Fortas thinks, I do give a damn that you are ass enough to believe that those stinkers are going to pay any attention to your high-class morals. It's tough for me to believe that you haven't recovered from that crap."

"What stinkers? The Committee?"

"Not only," he said. "You know very well what I am talking about. The Committee, the press, what you think are your friends, everybody. But to hell

with convincing you of anything sensible. Just remember there are rats in jail, and tough dikes, and
people who will push you hard just because they like
it, and guards who won't admire you, and food you
can't eat and unless you do eat it they'll put you in
solitary. You're headed for a good breakdown, if not
worse."

That conversation, a diary tells me, was to be repeated with variations many times during the next
week. But the next two days were the hardest for me;
I was not accustomed to doing what Hammett didn't
approve of and he knew it and counted on it. But on
the third day, tired of no sleep, I said, "Sorry. This
time I must do things my way."

There was no answer and I should have guessed
there wouldn't be.

I said, "And there is more bad news. The Internal Revenue won't let you have any more money,
I won't have any in a few years, so we'll have to sell
the farm."

"O.K.," he said cheerfully, "you'll live to have
another." (I haven't lived to have another and am too
old now to think that I could work a farm.)

But that day there were things to do. I called
Fortas to say that I had carefully decided that what he
had suggested was right for me. He said well, he
didn't know, he had to tell me that his partner thought
the whole idea rotten and calculated to send me
straight to jail.

I laughed. "Did he say it was liberal shit?"

"No," said Fortas, "he just thinks it's legal shit."

"I'd like to come to Washington, the sooner the better, and see the lawyer you spoke about."

Fortas arranged an appointment for me with Joseph Rauh for the next day. I took a night train to Washington, which was not a good idea; I still have odds and ends of notes from that rocky, no-sleep night. I should have been thinking of the House Committee, I guess, or worried about meeting Rauh. Instead I thought of the farm and how difficult it was going to be to tell Kitty, the housemaid, and Betty and Gus Benson, my farmers, that I couldn't keep the place anymore, and they had better look for new jobs. They were close to me, all three of them, and I remembered a scene only eight or nine months before that had made me know what good friends they were.

The day after Dash had gone to jail, I phoned the house to ask if there were reporters around the place. Yes, there were, the porch and lawn were filled with them. I said I wouldn't come home, I hoped they weren't too bothered, I would call again in a few days. I went to a hotel for three days and phoned again to the farm. No reporters now, nobody. I drove up from New York and asked the three of them to come and sit with me.

I said, "You know Mr. Hammett is in jail. That means it will be uncomfortable here for you, maybe more than uncomfortable. God knows what the FBI ant

During that time I put
ained Hammett and me
not speak about it once
moved about the house,
go on sale or go into
plans for the future —
hen I came out of jail.
a holiday on a sailboat,
shing trip, often a shack
, where he came from, so
buy it after a while. Once,
eeable, I even promised to
lands if he would agree to
the Louisiana bayous.

I started in the theatre at
e had met possibly four or
etween 1935 and 1952, but I
moved to Hollywood. During
he called me, said he was in
have dinner. That seemed odd,
alled me before. I didn't much
third and rather insistent in-
e. It was such a strange evening

or any other government agency will decide on now, and even if they don't do anything, you have a stuffy village to face."

Gus interrupted me to say that three FBI men had already been around to ask him a great number of questions. I wanted very much to find out what questions they had asked, but I knew Gus well enough to know that when he didn't volunteer to tell me, it meant that he was embarrassed and wanted to save my feelings. So I said that was the way things would probably be from now on, ugly, possibly even dangerous for them, and that I thought it would be better if . . . Before I could say better off in other jobs, Kitty laughed and said to Betty, "Tell Miss Hellman."

Betty said they had sent Hammett a telegram to West Street jail, congratulating him and sending him their love. Then Kitty giggled and said that in the next few days she and Betty would bake a cake and take it to him, but they were having an argument over what kind of cake, would I know what he would like? I was so moved by these nice people who had done what so many others — including the many, many people who owed Hammett money — had not dared to do that I covered my eyes.

Kitty said, "We're Irish, Miss Hellman. Jail's nothing." After a few minutes we all shook hands in a most formal manner and for a long time I could hear Kitty and Betty in the kitchen arguing about what kind of cake they would make for Hammett.

The following week they paid no attentio
warning to stay out of things, took the trair
York to deliver their coconut cake to the We
jail. They told me on their return that they
been allowed to see Dash, but two men said t
would be given to him. It wasn't, but I never tol

I LIKED RAUH. Shrewdness seldom goes wit
open nature, but in his case it does and the nice
beautiful, rugged, crinkly face gives one confid
about the mind above it. Our first meetings were
About the third time we met, Joe had evidently d
some research; he pointed out that the Commur
Party, sometimes through the *Daily Worker,* son
times in other publications, had attacked me. The
had been, for example, the nonsense about *Watch*
the Rhine. The play, opening before the Soviet Unio
was invaded by Germany, was reviewed as war
mongering. The movie, opening after the Soviet Union
was at war with Germany, was just wonderful. And
in 1948, when Tito broke with Russia, I had gone to
Belgrade and written a series of sympathetic inter-
views with Tito which were not well received by Communists here. Joe believed that we had to point out
these Communist criticisms of me because they would

ance before the Committee.
the farm up for sale. That
deeply, of course, but we di
we made the decision. As I
marking things that would
storage, Dash would make
the future meant to him
Sometimes we would plan
sometimes a three-month
on the shores of Maryland
cheap that maybe we could
when I was feeling too ag
go look at the Aleutian I
consider a crayfish farm i

CLIFFORD ODETS an
about the same time.
five times in the years
never saw him after he
the first week of Marcl
New York, couldn't we
since he had not ever
want to go, but on th
vitation we made a da

that I made a long entry in a diary for March 1952.
I copy it here:

We met at Barbetta's, ordered a dinner I guessed
right would be lousy, and a bad Italian wine. It didn't
take long to get to the reason for the dinner. Clifford
said, "Have you made plans for what you will do
when the House Committee calls you?"

I didn't intend to tell him that the Committee
had already called me. So I said, "I guess I have.
But you make plans and then just hope you can carry
them out, maybe, maybe not."

Clifford said something, but I couldn't hear him
because the man at the next table said to two other
men and a woman, "I was shaving. You know what?
She was so drunk that she thought her nipple was a
scar on her stomach."

"I never met her," said one of his companions.

"Easy to fix up if you don't mind 'em with nip-
ples on their stomach," said the first man.

I laughed. That must have annoyed Clifford because his voice was sharp. "You didn't hear what I
said."

"No. Sorry."

"I said that's a dangerous way to think. You
better damn well know what you're going to say and
do before you get there."

I didn't know how I was going to answer that,
but the waiter came with our dinner. Clifford put his

finger to his mouth to shush me and began to whistle until the waiter went away.

"What did you mean?"

"About what?" I was stalling. I didn't like the conversation.

"About not knowing what you're going to do when the Committee calls you?"

I said I hadn't said that, you may know what you're going to do, but you can't be sure what will happen to you under pressure.

"That's a strange way to think," Clifford said, "maybe because you've never been under pressure."

"But I have been. I was in Spain during their war, at the Russian front, in London during the V-2's —"

"Didn't you know how to act then?"

"Sometimes, sometimes not. Once I screamed for a good two minutes about a V-2 and couldn't stop myself, and once in Russia I was given a pair of binoculars to look out of a dugout window at the Germans a few hundred yards away and I held the glasses smack into the light and started a barrage from the Germans."

"That wasn't smart," Clifford said.

"That's exactly what I've been saying. It wasn't smart and it almost got six of us killed. That's what I'm trying to say, how can you know how stupid you'll be until you're stupid?"

He rapped on the table. Things weren't going

well. "I'm not talking about things like that. I'm talking about political and moral convictions."

I said, "I don't like to talk about convictions. I'm never sure I'm telling the truth."

"But Hammett has convictions," he said. "I don't know much about him, but I admire him."

I wanted to say that's nice but he doesn't admire you, remembering a night long ago when we had gone to see *Awake and Sing* and Hammett, very tipsy, had kept urging me to leave and we had left simply to keep him quiet. Once outside I said I liked the play, why didn't he, and he said, "Because I don't think writers who cry about not having had a bicycle when they were kiddies are ever going to amount to much."

But I said nothing, and Odets and I talked about his art collection for a while, and then suddenly he scared the hell out of me. He pounded on the table so hard that his wineglass spilled and he yelled, "Well, I can tell you what I am going to do before those bastards on the Committee. I am going to show them the face of a radical man and tell them to go fuck themselves." I don't know which impressed me most: the violence of the gesture on the table or the brave shout that turned heads at the tables near us.

I have no other diary notes for that night. But there is an unpleasant, mysterious ending to the story. Odets, who appeared before the Committee one day before I did, apologized for his old beliefs and identified many of his old friends as Communists. Therefore I don't understand that conversation in Barbetta's. It is possible that on that night he believed what he told me. One can only guess that a few weeks later, faced with the ruin of a Hollywood career, he changed his mind. The old clichés were now increasingly true; the loss of a swimming pool, a tennis court, a picture collection, future deprivation, were powerful threats to many people, and the heads of studios knew it and played heavy with it.

A few weeks after my dinner with Odets, Elia Kazan, whom everybody called Gadge, told me that Spyros Skouras had told him that unless he became what was called a "friendly witness" for the Committee, he, Kazan, would never make another movie in Hollywood. But before he told me anything that simple, we had spent a strange half-hour in the Plaza Oak Room. I couldn't understand what Gadge was fumbling with — he is not a fumbler — so on the excuse of having to make a phone call, I did make one to Kermit Bloomgarden, my theatre producer and the producer of *Death of a Salesman*, which Kazan had directed. (Kermit and Gadge had known each other since they were young, but I had never known Kazan well.) I told Kermit on the phone that I didn't know why Kazan had asked me for a drink, and I didn't understand what he was trying to tell me.

"He is telling you that he is going to become a friendly witness. I know because he told me this morning."

When I returned from the phone we talked for a few minutes and I invented a pressing engagement. We stood in front of the Plaza in the rain waiting for a taxi. I didn't want to talk anymore and so we stood in silence until Kazan said, "It's O.K. for you to do what you want, I guess. You've probably spent whatever you've earned."

This puzzled me for weeks afterwards until I figured out that he was really saying what my rich grandmother used to tell her less well-heeled friends or relatives, and I had once heard her say to her chauffeur, a man whose name she had changed from Fritz to Hal, "You don't have anything to worry about. Money doesn't put heavy burdens on those who don't have it."

But the panic of movie bosses was an old story by the time Kazan and I met in the spring of 1952. It had started even earlier than their famous meeting at the Waldorf-Astoria Hotel in 1947. There they came together in a kind of sleepy hysteria, called together by forces no amount of research can positively name even today, to assure the public, in a statement of massive confusions, that they most certainly believed in the American right to dissent, but that they were not going to allow dissent if they didn't like it. It used to be said that there was nothing like a studio lawyer except another studio lawyer.

(It was probably at this Waldorf conference that what later became known in Hollywood as the

American Legion oath was decided upon. The oath was to be demanded of studio employees. It seems obvious from its name that representatives of the American Legion must have been present in some form, either in person or, more likely, by visits before and after the Waldorf conference. I have made fourteen attempts to find a sample of these famous letters that I know exist because I was asked to sign one. None of the fourteen people I asked deny the letters were demanded and complied with. But no amount of digging has turned up one letter, possibly because those who wrote them don't want to admit they did and because the present studio legal departments don't like them much anymore, may even doubt their legality. I have come up with only one fact: each studio asked its employees to write letters swearing they were not Communists, did not associate with radicals, and if they had in the past contributed to certain organizations — aid to Spanish refugees, etc. — they regretted it and would not repeat the mistake.)

I don't think the heads of movie companies, and the men they appointed to run the studios, had ever before thought of themselves as American citizens with inherited rights and obligations. Many of them had been born in foreign lands and inherited foreign fears. It would not have been possible in Russia or Poland, but it was possible here to offer the Cossacks a bowl of chicken soup. And the Cossacks in Washington were now riding so fast and hard that the soup had to have double strength and be handed up by running millionaire waiters.

But long before the studios were threatened by politicians and the American Legion, their general timidity had been a joke for writers and directors who told each other nice stories about whose twelve-year-old son, whose eighteen-year-old mistress, had said they didn't like the script, or the rough cut of a movie, and thus the script or the rough cut had to be changed about. There had been, for example, in the late 1930's, a famous crisis at Metro-Goldwyn-Mayer. They had taken one of their big musicals to San Francisco for a sneak preview. It was then as it is now the custom to hand out postcards for the audience to fill out, asking their opinion of the picture they had just seen. One postcard writer loved the picture but wrote that she was horrified that Frank Morgan, an actor in the picture, had his fly wide open during one of his scenes. The postcard caused such consternation that the picture's opening was postponed and for a week all workers in the studio, coming to the projection room in craft groups, were shown the picture several times a day, and a prize was offered to anyone who could find Mr. Morgan's open fly. It was later discovered, obviously because so great a heroine couldn't keep her mouth shut, that the postcard had been written by a discarded mistress of a Metro official.

It is well to remember what these very rich movie men were like, since I doubt they have changed. (They have, indeed, increased in number, because agents often now outstrip them in money and power.) Hollywood lived the way the Arabs are attempting to live now, and while there is nothing strange about people vying with each other for great landed estates, there is something odd about people vying with each other for better bathrooms. It is doubtful that such luxury has ever been associated with the normal acts of defecating or bathing oneself. It is even possible that feces are not pleased to be received in such grand style and thus prefer to settle in the soul.

And in those days it was heady stuff to boss around William Faulkner or Nathanael West or Aldous Huxley. Gatsby and his ambitions were peanuts next to those larger Gatsbys; they didn't want love or Daisy, they wanted power and a new Daisy every week. But the natures of Louis Mayer, Samuel Goldwyn, Harry Cohn, and so on, their advisers and lawyers, are really not very interesting; they were one man with minor variations and quirks. Certainly they had force and daring, but by the time of McCarthy they had grown older and wearier. Threats that might once have been laughed about over a gin rummy game now seemed dangerous to their fortunes. Movie producers knew full well that the Communists of Hollywood had never made a single Communist picture, but they were perfectly willing to act as dupes for those who pretended that was a danger. Thousands of letters poured into Hollywood protesting Hollywood radicalism; the studios knew they were almost all faked or written to order. But they told themselves the voice of America was speaking, and to some extent it was. But the tycoons were not alone in cringing before threats that could have been investigated and forgotten. Harry Cohn told me that he was pleased at how many writers, directors and actors had volunteered to help. And he was telling the truth: there was a rush to be a helpful witness, to testify against one's associates, to act out the dramas that the government committees preferred.

In any case, the blacklist was not as yet completely operative in 1947 because Harry Cohn of Columbia Pictures offered me the contract I had always wanted: to write and produce four pictures any time I found a story I liked, and with control over the final cut. (This was almost unheard of in those days, and even now is seldom granted.) It was a fine contract: to write and produce without interference, at any time during eight years that I found the material I wanted to do. I was guaranteed almost a million dollars and I was free to write plays or anything else, to travel between jobs without questions asked. Harry and I had the same lawyer, Charles Schwartz, but that was O.K. because Charlie was an honest man. The day the contract was ready Charlie called me, said he was sending the copies up to Harry, would I go round and read them with Harry?

Charlie said, "I should warn you. Harry may

have attached a new piece of paper. He had to do it
and I advise you not to make a fuss. It will be re-
quired of everybody from now on."

I jumped to the conclusion that the new clause
had to do with money and forgot about it.

When I got to Harry's Waldorf Towers apartment, his secretary said he'd be up in a few minutes,
they were winding up the meeting downstairs. I didn't,
of course, know what meeting she meant; you always
wait for movie people to come from a meeting. Harry
did appear about a half-hour later, greeted me warmly,
went immediately to the telephone. He was still there
when I came upon a paragraph attached to the contract. I skipped it in disbelief, went on reading, went
back to read it again. Harry was making a new phone
call when I began to pace the room. But he was watching me, and I had a feeling he was staying on the
phone to avoid me, because he pointed to a desk,
held up a pen, made motions about signing, and went
back to the phone. When, finally, he was finished I
said, "The terms are O.K., Harry, just as we agreed,
but what does that new mishmash attachment mean?"

"Listen," he said, "do you think I like the two
days I've wasted downstairs? I'm a loner. I don't
like dictatorship. So let up on me, will you?"

I said I didn't know what he was talking about,
what meeting downstairs, but we were interrupted by
another telephone call and then by a waiter with a
thermos of hot milk and a chicken sandwich — I

don't remember Cohn without a chicken sandwich —
and a good many anecdotes of his past, in an effort,
I thought, to avoid the present. The present didn't
please Harry much: the meeting downstairs where, he
told me, every studio head in Hollywood had come to
town to decide that every employee had to compose
and sign a version of the letter clause I had just read.
Harry did, that day, in a garble of irritation, mention the American Legion, and "men" from Washington, exhibitors, bankers and their lawyers, lawyers
from "the Committees," and many others, perhaps
correctly identified, perhaps not, in his high state of
annoyance over being dictated to and bored. (I heard
later that he had raised no protest at the meeting itself. Samuel Goldwyn was the only producer who
refused to agree with his colleagues. One would like
to think it was a vote for freedom, but most people
who knew him well, I among them, knew that he always voted against any group decision.)

As Cohn talked I read and reread the attached
piece of paper. It asked that I write a note in my own
words and "suggested" a form of the old morals
clause — my actions, my life must not embarrass
the studios — but this time it didn't mean drunken-
ness or fights or murder, it meant simply that my politics must not embarrass them or cause them any
trouble or protests. (I am making it milder than it
was; it was, in truth, a straight demand that nothing
you believed, or acted upon, or contributed to, or

associated with could be different from what the studio would allow.) I started to make a speech about constitutional rights and who the hell did they think they were, but I was exhausted by Harry's troubles: he had called room service to say the chicken sandwich stank from dryness, two obviously unimportant telephone calls had been put through, and for five minutes a pretty girl had appeared from nowhere with nothing to say. I was tired now.

I said, "You know, Harry, I live with Dashiell Hammett. I don't think he is going to stay in the attic and be taken out on a chain at night."

"Fine writer," said Harry, "wanted to hire him for years."

"Call him," I said, "skip the fine writer junk and tell him about the attic."

"Ach," he said, "you're just looking for trouble."

"And there are many other people I know, intend to go on knowing, have dinner with —"

"So have dinner in some nice little place in Santa Monica. Better and cheaper than Romanoff's or Chasen's —"

I said, "Harry, I won't write such a letter. Please stop asking for it."

"I can't do that. They'd have my tail. Write it, sign the contract and forget it."

I said, "I won't sign it and you knew I wouldn't when I came here. It's a disgrace."

As I started for the door, Harry said, "You take

things too serious. Give me a call in the morning, kid."

I was not to see Harry Cohn again for nine or ten years, and then we met on a plane flying from Los Angeles to New York. He was, of course, the first to enter the plane, followed by six or seven men. When I passed him to take my seat, we shook hands and mumbled about how many years, and he said I got younger and he got older, and things like that. When it came time for lunch, he sent back an invitation for me to join him, saying that he had brought his own food, it was much healthier than the dreck on the plane. Two of his younger employees hauled down the largest picnic hamper I have ever seen. It was filled with forty or fifty fine, thin chicken sandwiches, cold white wine, prosciutto wrapped around perfect ripe melon, homemade pickles, large peaches, wonderful walnut cookies. The hamper held enough for twenty people, and Harry and I made no noticeable dent in it. When we finished, Harry called to somebody named Lou to bring the tea bottles, and when Lou appeared to close our hamper and to present another, he leaned over to take one of the many chicken sandwiches. Harry made a fist and brought it down hard on Lou's hand.

"The chutzpah," he said to me, "plain chutzpah," and to Lou he said, "Keep yourself in line, sonny."

I don't know whether sonny ever got out of line again because that was the last time I ever saw Cohn.

I can't remember when he died, but there was a nice story at the time, attributed to George Jessel. Jessel and a friend were standing outside the funeral parlor. The line of mourners was very long.

The friend said, "I never saw such a mob at a funeral."

Jessel said, "Same old story: you give 'em what they want and they'll fill the theatre."

IT IS IMPOSSIBLE to write about any part of the McCarthy period in a clear-dated, annotated form; much crossed with much else, nothing obeyed a neat plan. It is plain that the producers at the Waldorf meeting, called by "them," did not know how to carry out the plans that "them" forced upon them. And most of them didn't want to know; a strict observance would have meant loss of revenue on pictures already made and still unsold to television, loss of many talented people, unwanted involvement of many of their high money-makers. If one remembers that Gary Cooper, James Cagney, Frederic March, Humphrey Bogart were all at some point variously involved, even in the most innocent way, then what new nut might appear tomorrow with what new nut charge against whom? And the most militant fighters against the

Hollywood left, the mother of Ginger Rogers, Adolphe Menjou, and such, were getting too much attention, speaking too loud for comfort. Who knew what they might say tomorrow if they spoke with God's wild eye today? Maybe producers themselves, whose private lives had been as guarded as the men in the Kremlin, might come to the attention of a Representative or a Senator; what had been a noble half-hour romance might come to light or, much more important, a strange financial maneuver. Stockholders might, with enough talk even from people who meant well, see that the often fancy accounting books attached to movies included the price of old discarded scripts, limousines, vacations, or an extra, unreported yearly bonus. And many Hollywood witnesses, even the most sympathetic to the studios, weren't always acting with sense before the committees. Gary Cooper was asked, in a most deferential and friendly manner, if he had read much Communist propaganda in the scripts submitted to him. Cooper, as a man who had not been called upon ever to speak very much, thought that one over and said no, he didn't think he had, but then he mostly read at night. This puzzling answer caused too many giggles around the country and Cooper was not a man anybody should be giggling about. (And, much later on, there were to be shudders as well as laughter when Charles Laughton, who had been a close friend of Bertolt Brecht, received a cable from the East German government inviting

77

him to attend his old friend's memorial service. Mr. Laughton immediately phoned J. Edgar Hoover to say that he had received the wire, but after all that it wasn't his fault and shouldn't be counted against him.)

But many people who were questioned acted neither good nor bad, just puzzled. How could you know that during the war a benefit for Russian War Relief wasn't as irreproachable as Bundles for Britain? You couldn't possibly have guessed, unless you were mentally disturbed, that there would come into being such a phrase as "premature anti-Fascist." The popularity of that phrase, the fact that most of America took it seriously and even pretended to understand it, must have been the forerunner of the double-talk we were to hear in the Watergate days. We, as a people, agreed in the Fifties to swallow any nonsense that was repeated often enough, without examination of its meaning or investigation into its roots.

It is no wonder then that many "respectable," meaning friendly, witnesses were often bewildered by what was wanted of them, and that many, who were convinced by the surrounding hysterical pressures that they had something to hide, moved in a dream pavanne trying to guess what the committees wanted them to admit. They scratched around hard for dramatic revelations, inventing sins for the Inquisitor priests.

I told that to Mrs. Shipley, head of the Passport

Division of the State Department, in 1953. It was that year, after my own hearing, that I had an offer to do a movie script for the producer Alexander Korda, in London. The salary was a fifth of what I had earned before the blacklist, but we needed the money and it was no time to argue. (Korda was not the only producer who saw the chance to pick up practiced writers for little money, and the fact that he was to cheat me out of a third of the fifth that he had offered was only to come later.)

It was necessary, of course, to go to Europe to consult with Korda and to write the picture. Everybody who had appeared as an unfriendly witness had been denied a passport. Joe Rauh suggested that I go to see Mrs. Shipley. It seemed to me a useless visit, but Rauh thought I had a chance, and when I asked why, he said he'd tell me after I had seen her.

She was a severe-looking lady with a manner made more severe by its attempt not to be. We sat awkwardly in her office while a secretary was sent off for my file. I remember murmuring something about the weather and never finishing the sentence because Mrs. Shipley was staring at me. And so we sat silent for the few minutes it took the secretary to return with a fat folder. When Mrs. Shipley opened the folder I was amazed to see three large pictures of Charles Chaplin on top. I had known Chaplin, but not well, had played tennis on his court, had once listened to an endless script he wrote and never produced, had once been on a platform with him at a meeting and had been openly disapproving of his emotional, rambling speech, had once been at dinner with him and Gertrude Stein. I admired Chaplin and liked him, but to this day I do not know why his pictures were in my file. Government agencies in those wild days probably had even more misinformation than they have now, although that can always be remedied any time invention is needed again.

Mrs. Shipley did not comment on the Chaplin pictures, but began to read a list of organizations to which I had either belonged or contributed money, and a few I had never heard of. I wanted to say that I recognized the list as coming from a book called *Red Channels*, hardly a proper source for a government agency to be using. As she read down the list, there would have been no sense denying my connection with one organization and affirming the next, and so I sat silent wondering why I had sought out this degrading hour.

Mrs. Shipley had not finished the list when she looked up and said, "Tell me, Miss Hellman, do you think most of the friendly witnesses have been telling the House Un-American Committee the truth?"

It was a most surprising question. I said no, I was sure they had not, many of them had been coached to confess what they had never done and had never seen.

Mrs. Shipley said, "Edward G. Robinson, for example?"

I said I thought so, but I wasn't sure. But there were others, Martin Berkeley for example, who said that I had been at a Communist meeting in his house. I was never at his house and didn't believe I ever met him.

I said, "The kiddies have been playing games on all of you, Mrs. Shipley, and you deserve the tricks they played because you pushed them into it."

Mrs. Shipley did not seem angry. She was thoughtful as she riffled through the rest of my file, seemingly looking for something she knew was there. Then she said, "I've suspected many of them were lying. They will be punished for it."

I said, "I don't think that's the way the world is going. It's people like me who need jobs. That's why I came here, not wanting to come."

She said, "I can see that," and was close to a smile. When the near smile had been suppressed she said, "When you go to Europe do you see political people?"

I said I didn't know many, except Louis Aragon and his wife Elsa Triolet, and a few men who had fought in Spain.

She said, "Please write me a letter saying that and that you will take no part in political movements."

I thought about that for a while, not understanding it, looking for the trick. Then I said, "I've never had any part in European political movements, except to be anti-Nazi and anti-Fascist. Certainly I'll write you just that. But I can't promise not to see old friends."

She rose. "Thank you." She moved toward the door. "You will be issued a limited passport. It will be sent to you this week. If you wish to stay in Europe longer because of your cinema work, you will have to apply here again."

She went out of the room. A secretary appeared and opened another door for me into the hall from which I had entered. Rauh was waiting on a bench.

He got up. "You got the passport."

"Yes."

As we left the building, he grinned. "I think you're the only unfriendly witness who has gotten one."

"Why were you so sure I would get it? Certainly I didn't think so."

"Because," he said, "one Puritan lady in power recognized another Puritan lady in trouble. Puritan ladies have to believe that other Puritan ladies don't lie."

But all that was months after I appeared before the Committee.

Two DAYS AGO, in the writing of this book, I was sitting on Gay Head beach in Martha's Vineyard, eating a sandwich, with a pile of magazines I hadn't been able to catch up on. As in all places where you've lived for a long time, I had been saying hello to people whose names I couldn't remember, and hoping they wouldn't stop long enough for them to know that I couldn't. Two middle-aged people did stop to talk, to ask me what I was writing, a question that irritates me so much that I deny I am doing anything. The man, who didn't like my answer, pointed to a copy of the *New York Review of Books* and said, "In that case you must read Lionel Trilling's piece about Whittaker Chambers. Maybe you'll want to write a history of your times."

I laughed and said I wasn't a historian. But when they had passed I did pick up the piece, which was in too old an issue to include yesterday's news that the only things that had been found in Chambers's pumpkin were five rolls of microfilm, two developed, three in metal containers, most of the frames were unreadable, none of them had anything to do with the charges against Alger Hiss. And yet one remembers Mr. Nixon holding them up for the camera, saying here was documentary evidence of the most serious series of treasonable activities which had been launched against the government in the history of America. But Nixon is a villainous liar. Lionel

Trilling, a distinguished critic and teacher, an early anti-Communist, the author of a novel roughly based on the career of Whittaker Chambers, is an honest man.

I suddenly wanted to go home and did, to spend the rest of the day asking myself how Diana and Lionel Trilling, old, respected friends, could have come out of the same age and time with such different political and social views from my own.

Facts are facts — and one of them is that a pumpkin, in which Chambers claimed to have hidden the damaging evidence against Hiss, deteriorates — and there never had been a chance that, as Trilling continues to claim in the *New York Review*, Chambers was a man of honor. The youthful psychotic inventions of Chambers were talked about in almost undeniable terms by those who knew him better than Trilling in Washington and New York, and later by men who had worked with him on *Time* magazine. But I told myself that Chambers was an unimportant part of an important puzzle. If facts are facts, and should not be altered, then which of us, as individuals or in groups, did the alterations and why? To many intellectuals the radicals had become the chief, perhaps the only, enemy. (There had been a history of this that preceded my generation: Eugene Debs had been hounded into jail by Woodrow Wilson, and there had been the vicious trials of the men of the International Workers of the World.) Not alone because the radical's intellectual reasons were suspect, but because his convictions would lead to a world that deprived the rest of us of what we had. Very few people are capable of admitting anything so simple: the radical had to be made into an immoral man who justified murder, prison camps, torture, any means to an end. And, in fact, he sometimes was just that. But the anti-radical camp contained the same divisions: often they were honest and thoughtful men, often they were men who turned down a dark road for dark reasons.

But radicalism or anti-radicalism should have had nothing to do with the sly, miserable methods of McCarthy, Nixon and colleagues, as they flailed at Communists, near-Communists, and nowhere-near-Communists. Lives were being ruined and few hands were raised in help. Since when do you have to agree with people to defend them from injustice? Certainly nobody in their right mind could have believed that the China experts, charged and fired by the State Department, did any more than recognize that Chiang Kai-shek was losing. Truth made you a traitor as it often does in a time of scoundrels. But there were very few who stood up to say so and there are almost none even now to remind us that one of the reasons we know so little and guess so badly about China is that we lost the only men who knew what they were talking about. Certainly the good magazines, the ones that published the most serious writers, should have come to the aid of those who were persecuted. *Partisan Review,* although through the years it has published many pieces protesting the punishment of dissidents in Eastern Europe, made no protest when people in this country were jailed or ruined. In fact, it never took an editorial position against McCarthy himself, although it did publish the results of anti-McCarthy symposiums and at least one distinguished piece by Irving Howe. *Commentary* didn't do anything. No editor or contributor ever protested against McCarthy. Indeed, Irving Kristol in that magazine wrote about McCarthy's critics, Henry Steele Commager among others, as if they were naughty children who needed Kristol to correct their innocence.

There were many thoughtful and distinguished men and women on both magazines. None of them, as far as I know, has yet found it a part of conscience to admit that their Cold War anti-Communism was perverted, possibly against their wishes, into the Vietnam War and then into the reign of Nixon, their unwanted but inevitable leader.

T̲HAT WAS a tough spring, 1952. There were not alone the arrangements for my appearance before the Committee, there were other kinds of trouble. Hammett owed the Internal Revenue a great deal of back taxes: two days after he went to jail they attached all income from books, radio or television, from anything. He was, therefore, to have no income for the remaining ten years of his life. I myself had been badly advised about the movie sale of a play, and although "Washington" — meaning the then director of Internal Revenue — had given his unofficial O.K. at the time of the sale, the department now changed its mind and claimed I owed them a hundred and seventy-five thousand dollars. I had insisted upon taking Hammett's conviction and prison sentence — against his will, and without his cooperation — to the Court of Appeals and that had cost money, a lot of it, and certainly my own new troubles would be expensive. And we would both now be totally banned in Hollywood or television or radio. The money was going, would be going faster, and I was floundering around for decisions about how to live, what to do without, knowing that Hammett was ill and not knowing from day to day what would be needed for him. I don't remember whether worries like that led to Rauh's asking for a postponement of my appearance, or whether he needed time to think about the legal problems. I quote from a memorandum Rauh sent me, this July, 1975. The memorandum is dated March 26, 1952.

This morning I saw Tavenner, Chief Counsel of the House Un-American Committee. . . . After some rather forced pleasantries I explained the purpose of my visit. . . . I asked Tavenner what it was the Committee was particularly interested in. He said the Committee had received sworn testimony that Miss Hellman had been a member of the Communist Party and the Committee wanted to go into that subject. I said that I was not in a position to indicate whether Miss Hellman had ever been a member of the Communist Party, but I was in a position to state that she was prepared to tell the Committee about her activities in all organizations. They seemed so delighted with this that I went right on to point out the legal dilemma involved. . . . If Miss Hellman answered questions about herself she could legally be compelled to answer questions about others; and this she could not morally do. . . . They indicated sympathy but nothing more. . . . He (Tavenner) . . . mentioned that Budd Schulberg had initially refused to name anybody, but subsequently had been persuaded to change his position. He seemed to feel that Miss Hellman, too, would be persuaded. . . . [He] asked me whether I thought Miss Hellman would be more likely to name people in executive (private) session . . . indicating a willingness to talk to Miss Hellman prior to the hearing. . . . Tavenner said this was more for Miss Hellman's benefit . . . as it would make it easier for her to get her dates straight. . . . Nixon [the Committee's research director, not Richard] said they were doing the "entire entertainment field" and were particularly interested in the "literary field" to show how the Communist Party sought to control the thinking of its members. Tavenner asked me if Miss Hellman had any experience with efforts by the Communist Party to dictate her writings. I said Miss Hellman is an individualist . . . [and] I would like to point out that *Watch on the Rhine* had been written in 1940 when Communists were supposed to be pro, not anti, Nazi. They asked me how I could explain Miss Hellman writing an anti-party-line play at this time. . . . The meet-

ing more or less broke up on the note that Miss Hellman
was a maverick and they would be as nice as they could
but there was no way of avoiding naming other people.

I have no memory of Joe's ever telling me of this
meeting. I think I knew about it first in his letter of
this July. I am sure that Rauh had to have the meeting, but it is the proof that as much as we liked each
other then and now, there was a good part of me he
never understood. Perhaps it is fairer to say that
whenever I am making a great effort to control myself, I do act in a peculiar manner, and he is not the
first who has been bewildered. But, as I have written,
I did not want to use the attacks of the Communist
Party on me; in my thin morality book it is plain not
cricket to clear yourself by jumping on people who
are themselves in trouble. Most of the Communists I
had met seemed to me people who wanted to make a
better world; many of them were silly people and a
few of them were genuine nuts, but that doesn't make
for denunciation or furnish enough reason for turning
them over for punishment to men who wanted nothing
more than newspaper headlines that could help their
own careers. The greatest mistakes made by native
Communists came from their imitation of Russians, a
different breed of people with a totally different history. American Communists accepted Russian theory
and practice with the enthusiasm of a lover whose
mistress cannot complain because she speaks few

words of his language; that may be the mistress many men dream about, but it is for bed and not for politics. Nor did they realize that as children of their time and place, they mixed idealism with the unattractive rules of the marketplace: gain, loss, fame, and a kind of comic secrecy borrowed from the directors of giant corporations. Communist-haters, particularly among intellectuals, wrote and talked a good deal about the violence they could suffer at the hands of American Communists — Whittaker Chambers sold a bill of goods on that romantic theme — but I think that was a very doubtful charge. About foreign gunmen I know only what I have read, but the American radicals I met were not violent men.

It is hard to believe, for example, that anybody could have thought of V. J. Jerome, the theoretician of the Party, as a man with a bomb or a gun. I didn't know Jerome very well, but one night, I think in the hope of convincing me that the Party had its high culture side, he insisted upon reading aloud and interpreting Shelley's *The Cenci*. During the last half I took the dog for a walk and if Jerome knew I was missing, he didn't mention it on my return. Years later, Jerome and several other Communist officials were in West Street jail at the same time Hammett was there. Hammett told me of an incident I like. There was a ping-pong table on the roof of the jail and one afternoon Hammett was playing partners with Jerome against one man who had been arrested for murdering a federal agent and one who was in for armed bank robbery. Jerome insisted the possible murderer had called a bad shot when it was really good. Hammett suggested that maybe Jerome shouldn't expect honesty from criminals. Jerome had held up the game to explain to Dash the socialist necessity to believe in the reform of all men, the duty to show them the honest way. When they resumed the game with their impatient partners, all seemed to go better until about the tenth shot, when Jerome shouted across the table that the murderer had cheated again and that he was shocked. The murderer threw his bat across the table and advanced on Jerome with a knife. Hammett said, "Mr. Jerome wishes to apologize."

Jerome said, "I do not wish to apologize. You should be ashamed of yourself for cheating a jailed comrade. You must learn —"

As the knife was thrown, Hammett pushed Jerome to the floor and held on to the murderer with repeated apologies that hinted Jerome wasn't all there in the head. Peace was restored when Hammett made Jerome buy the knife-thrower two packs of cigarettes and take an oath not to play ping-pong again. Maybe Jerome's Russian counterpart would have been dangerous, but then his Russian counterpart might also have been less silly.

The intellectuals who joined the Party, and then left it, had a right to object to the extraordinary language that the faithful used to attack them. But only literary people can confuse shouts of "renegade" or "traitor" with the damage of a gun or a bomb.

IN APRIL of 1952 I put the Pleasantville farm up for sale, and the shock of that may be the reason I have so little memory, and almost no notes, for the few weeks before my appearance before the Committee. I know, of course, that Rauh wrote a letter that I was to send to the Committee; I didn't like it much because it didn't sound like me. Then I wrote a version, he wrote another, I rewrote him, he rewrote me, and we came out with the version that I quote here.

May 19, 1952

Honorable John S. Wood
Chairman
House Committee on Un-American Activities
Room 226 Old House Office Building
Washington 25, D.C.

Dear Mr. Wood:

As you know, I am under subpoena to appear before your Committee on May 21, 1952.

I am most willing to answer all questions about myself. I have nothing to hide from your Committee and there is nothing in my life of which I am ashamed. I have been

1935: The author of The Children's Hour.

*Lillian Hellman and Dashiell Hammett,
Pleasantville, the late 1940's.*

WIDE WORLD PHOTO

Inside the Waldorf: Shostakovich and L.H. at the Cultural and Scientific Conference for World Peace, March 1949.

EORGE SILK/TIME-LIFE PICTURE AGENCY © TIME, INC.

Outside the Waldorf: picketing, March 1949.

UNITED PRESS INTERNATIONAL PHOTO

*The House Commit-
tee on Un-American
Activities, 1948:
Chairman J. Parnell
Thomas second
from left, Represen-
tative Richard M.
Nixon at far right.*

WIDE WORLD PHOTOS

Richard M. Nixon, Whittaker Chambers (at left) and Committee Counsel Robert Stripling, 1948.

NEW YORK DAILY NEWS PHOTO

Dashiell Hammett on the way to jail, 1951.

WALTER F. DARAN/TIME-LIFE PICTURE AGENCY Ⓒ TIME, INC.

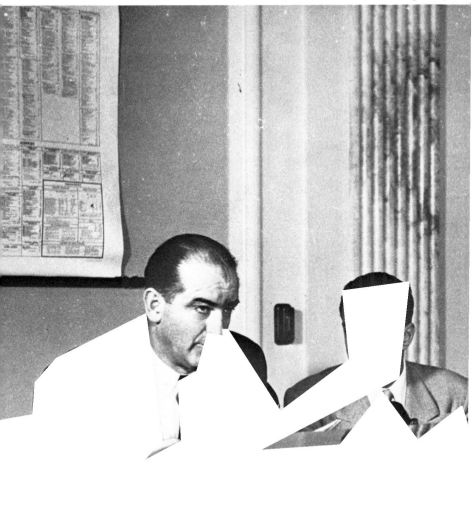

Senator Joseph McCarthy and Roy Cohn.

HANK WALKER/TIME-LIFE PICTURE AGENCY © TIME, INC.

Dashiell Hammett testifying before the Senate Internal Security Subcommittee,
1953.

RICHARD DE COMBRAY

1975: The author of Scoundrel Time.

advised by counsel that under the Fifth Amendment I have a constitutional privilege to decline to answer any questions about my political opinions, activities and associations, on the grounds of self-incrimination. I do not wish to claim this privilege. I am ready and willing to testify before the representatives of our Government as to my own opinions and my own actions, regardless of any risks or consequences to myself.

But I am advised by counsel that if I answer the Committee's questions about myself, I must also answer questions about other people and that if I refuse to do so, I can be cited for contempt. My counsel tells me that if I answer questions about myself, I will have waived my rights under the Fifth Amendment and could be forced legally to answer questions about others. This is very difficult for a layman to understand. But there is one principle that I do understand: I am not willing, now or in the future, to bring bad trouble to people who, in my past association with them, were completely innocent of any talk or any action that was disloyal or subversive. I do not like subversion or disloyalty in any form and if I had ever seen any I would have considered it my duty to have reported it to the proper authorities. But to hurt innocent people whom I knew many years ago in order to save myself is, to me, inhuman and indecent and dishonorable. I cannot and will not cut my conscience to fit this year's fashions, even though I long ago came to the conclusion that I was not a political person and could have no comfortable place in any political group.

I was raised in an old-fashioned American tradition and there were certain homely things that were taught to me: to try to tell the truth, not to bear false witness, not to harm my neighbor, to be loyal to my country, and so on. In general, I respected these ideals of Christian honor and did as well with them as I knew how. It is my belief that you will agree with these simple rules of human decency and will not expect me to violate the good American tradition from which they spring. I would, therefore, like to come before you and speak of myself.

I am prepared to waive the privilege against self-incrimination and to tell you anything you wish to know about my views or actions if your Committee will agree to refrain from asking me to name other people. If the Committee is unwilling to give me this assurance, I will be forced to plead the privilege of the Fifth Amendment at the hearing.

A reply to this letter would be appreciated.

Sincerely yours,

LILLIAN HELLMAN

NOTES FROM A DIARY. May 16, 1952.

Meg maybe started it all. She jumped on my bed at five this morning. She never does this, being too proud ever to need me or anything else. I've loved this dog since I helped pull her from her mother, but now I kicked her and she went away somewhere and wouldn't eat her breakfast. Leaving the house, I bump into Maggie, who was trying to sweep the hall. She's drunk, early, as usual, but the FBI has twice examined her about me and she's drunker now than before they came.

The Shoreham Hotel, Washington. Why have I come down here this early and without telling anybody? I'll call Hammett tonight and tell him where I am. The phone will be tapped but what difference does it make. No, I won't call him. I'll go buy some magazines and order caviar and steak, and go to sleep. The steak was bad and there wasn't any caviar. I'm going to spend a lot of money on something tomorrow.

May 17th. I've just come back from looking at expensive dresses, buying nothing. I'm growing scared about money and this is the week I must not. There'll be plenty of years for that kind of thing, but this week I will pretend I don't know it. I phoned Dash and told him where I was. He said he thought he had better come down and I said he wasn't to. We've been over all this so many times before. He could do nothing but harm me here, his name, I mean, and anyway, I don't want to think about his disapproval of what I'm doing. I called Joe, didn't say I was in Washington, asked him if he needed me. He said he didn't but to keep in touch. Keep in touch is a funny phrase, I don't think I've ever said it.

May 18th. I never should have come. I haven't anything to do with myself. I'll go to the National Gallery. I hate this neighborhood: no place to walk, refined.

Night. I didn't go to the National Gallery. I went to the zoo. Nice to see living things that don't know anything about future troubles or death or Committees. I've always wanted to go to bed with an orangou-

tan, but I guess I never will. I now have a taxi driver
who waits for me, without charge, because he says he
doesn't feel cheerful. I called Dash. He said he was
eating a lamb chop. I told him about me and the
orangoutan and he said maybe he'd call me back after
he ate his lamb chop.

May 19th. I bought a beautiful, expensive Balmain. It will make me feel better to wear it. Then I
went to Harvey's for lunch and the waiter pointed out
J. Edgar Hoover and Clyde Tolson and said they came
to lunch every day. I bet they have an orangoutan
every night. But I leave my lunch after I see them: a
nasty pair. My cab driver is waiting and I decide to
take a plane to New York, come back on the 20th.
But halfway to the airport, I change my mind.

May 20th. In a sleepless night, I realize why I
came to Washington earlier than I needed to. Five
days ago I went to Lennie Bernstein's for dinner. It
was a pleasant dinner with Shirley and a couple
whose name I heard and forgot. After dinner Harry
comes in. [Note of 1975: I have changed his name;
he is an old man now, and his appearance before
the Committee broke his life into poverty and ill
health.] Everybody wants to hear Harry talk because
two weeks ago he appeared as an unfriendly witness
before the House Com. I am, of course, particularly
anxious to listen, although nobody in the room knows
that I will appear in the next week. Harry, of course,
enjoys the attention and admiration, and I like him

for that. Or I like him until he says that his lawyer
made him memorize the answers to twenty-five questions before his appearance. That scares me good.
Rauh has coached me in nothing. Somebody asks,
"How did your lawyer know what twenty-five they
would ask?"

"He took the odds," said Harry, "based on what
he'd seen and heard with other people."

I hear myself say, "I couldn't learn the answers
to any twenty-five questions and I won't."

I feel sick and I go home. I phone Joe. "You
didn't tell me I had to learn the answers to lots of
questions. I can't do that and you should have told
me." Joe said he didn't know what I was talking
about. I told him about Harry and he asked who had
been Harry's lawyer. Before I could say I didn't
know, Joe said he didn't believe Harry, that maybe
Harry was O.K. in other ways, but he wasn't telling
the truth. Everybody had a right to make themselves a
little more heroic, maybe I would do it, too; then he
laughed and said no, I couldn't, the chances were the
other way, get a night's sleep, there was nothing to
memorize: he did have two pieces of advice to give
me, nothing important, and better for the last minute.

I guess Harry was the reason I wanted to get out
of New York.

One day more to go. I phoned Rauh, who is out,
and left a message that I am at the Shoreham. Then
I go with my taxi driver to pick up my new dress. I

buy a very expensive hat and a fine pair of white kid gloves. On the way back to the hotel with my packages I ask the taxi driver if he could pick me up at eight the next morning. He says sure, it would take his mind off things. What things? His wife has cancer of the throat, but they won't do the operation before noon. That's all he said, all I said. Before I left him, I gave him a check for a hundred dollars and asked him to buy his wife a present. I'd like to think it was generous of me: it was more maybe if I'm a good girl now God will help me and stuff like that. My dress, my hat, my gloves, my gift will be the last extravagances for many years. They felt good. There were two *New York Times* in my room, one of today, one from yesterday. I hadn't wanted to read them and I was, instinctively, right: Clifford Odets had testified as a friendly witness, throwing in the names of old friends and associates. His old friend Elia Kazan had done the same thing a month before and followed it up with an advertisement in the *New York Times* that is hard to believe for its pious shit. I sat for a long time thinking about Clifford, the dinner at Barbetta's: had he meant what he told me that night or had it all been a put-on. Maybe worse — an attempt to find out what I would do or say. It is impossible to think that a grown man, intelligent, doesn't have some sense of how he will act under pressure. It's all been decided so long ago, when you are very young, all mixed up with your childhood's definition of pride or dignity.

I think this is why I don't like Joe's occasional doubts about whether I will change my position once I am in the Committee room; I may make an ass of myself, but that will be all. Under special circumstances, torture, for example, people will and should break. I remember Louis Aragon telling me, and Camus repeating it the only time I ever met him, that the French underground during the war were given orders to hold out against torture as long as they could, so that others might have time to escape, but not to die or be crippled under torture, to give in and talk. That makes sense. But nobody here has been tortured and I don't like the fashionable case made out for mental torture being equal to broken arms and burned tongues. To hell with it. I need sleep.

THE LETTER THAT I SENT the Committee on May 19, 1952, had been refused by letter on May 20. It was, therefore, necessary for me to do what I did not want to do: take the Fifth Amendment. The Fifth Amendment is, of course, a wise section of the Constitution: you cannot be forced to incriminate yourself. But the amendment has difficulties that are hard for a layman to understand. Both Rauh and I believed that my wartime trip to Russia, about which I have written in another book, would be the center of the Committee's questions. In 1944 the Russians had invited me to visit the USSR as a kind of cultural representative. Both President Roosevelt and Harry Hopkins thought that was a good idea, but, understandably, did not want to endorse it as an official trip. My flight across Siberia had been arranged by the Russians, but Charles Bohlen of the State Department had evidently been instructed to get me as far as Alaska. In Moscow I had stayed for months in the embassy as the guest of Averell Harriman, who was our ambassador. Both Rauh and I believed that the Committee would ask me about that visit in their open antagonism to the Roosevelt period. The Fifth Amendment has catches: if I were asked if I knew Harriman or President Roosevelt, I would have to say yes because I could not claim that knowing them could harm me; but if I were asked if I knew Chaplin or Hammett, for example, I would have to refuse to answer because they could, in the eyes of the Committee, incriminate me. Thus, of course, one puts a finger on certain people and possibly on people about whom you know little and whose history you can only guess at. Maybe it is all legally necessary, well thought out, but it can be ugly stuff in practice.

My hearing was scheduled for eleven o'clock on the morning of May 21, 1952. Rauh had asked me to be at his office at eight-thirty. I tried to sleep, failed, tried to read, took two hot baths. Twice the phone had rung and, believing it was Hammett, I decided not to answer because I knew he would see through any pretend voice or manner. I tried during the night to find out what was going on in me — "thinking things out" was the voice of my time — and gave that up toward dawn in a kind of nasty amusement that the time for self-examination was over; calm had set in because I've known all my life that a show of temper, or even an ordinary set of jitters, once it starts, cannot be stopped and thus cannot begin. And so I had a big breakfast, and took my sad taxi driver to Joe's office. We shook hands and he said he would come and tell me about his wife. I gave him my New York address, but I never heard from him again.

Rauh was on the telephone. He nodded at me, put his hand over the phone, said he was talking to Thurman Arnold (Arnold had been an Assistant Attorney General and was now a partner of Abe Fortas). Rauh's usually cheerful face was set and stern. I picked up a newspaper, went into another room, read for a few minutes, and looked up to see Rauh standing in the doorway.

He said, "Thurman Arnold called me. He says that I am sending you straight to jail with the letter we wrote. He says he believes that we must find a way to say we have changed our mind about the letter before the hearing starts. His exact words were,

'You and Fortas are making a martyr of this woman.'
I don't want to make a martyr of you. Arnold is a very
fine lawyer."

I got up and went down the hall, walked up and
down, tried a locked door of the ladies' room, thinking
I needed to be sick. Rauh, with the best will, had upset
me to the point of sickness. I cannot make quick turns,
cannot even take a plane in the afternoon if I have
counted on flying in the morning, cannot ever adjust
fast to a new pattern, have not the mind or the nature
to do one thing, maybe wiser, when I am prepared
for another. I wanted to tell Rauh that I was angry
with him, that the nerves I had been controlling with
some kind of discipline were about to go to pieces.
But when I came back into his office he looked so
miserable that I could say none of that.

I said, "Please call Mr. Arnold and thank him
for me. But tell him that whatever happens to me now
will be better than what could happen if we start anything new. And then you stop feeling guilty because
that's bad for me this morning."

Rauh, his assistant Daniel Pollitt, and I took a
taxi to the Old House Office Building. I remember
saying to myself, "Just make sure you come out un-
ashamed. That will be enough."

Joe tapped me on the arm. "If things get too
much for you, tell me and I'll tell the Committee you
have to go to the ladies' room. You can probably do
that only once, so take your time, wash your face,

have a cigarette. If you don't need a rest, then keep your eye on the clock and remember that they'll take a lunch break around twelve-thirty. We may be called back, of course, but you'll have at least an hour and a half for a nap or a drink or both. Now this is more important so listen carefully: *don't make jokes.*"

"Make *jokes?* Why would I make jokes?"

"Almost everybody, when they feel insulted by the Committee, makes a joke or acts smart-aleck. It's a kind of embarrassment. Don't do it."

The Committee room was almost empty except for a few elderly, small-faced ladies sitting in the rear. They looked as if they were permanent residents and, since they occasionally spoke to each other, it was not too long a guess that they came as an organized group or club. Clerks came in and out, put papers on the rostrum, and disappeared. I said maybe we had come too early, but Joe said no, it was better that I get used to the room.

Then, I think to make the wait better for me, he said, "Well, I can tell you now that in the early days of seeing you, I was scared that what happened to my friend might happen to me."

He stopped to tell Pollitt that he didn't understand about the press — not one newspaperman had appeared.

I said, "What happened to your friend?"

"He represented a Hollywood writer who told him that he would under no circumstances be a friendly witness. That was why my friend took the case. So they get here, in the same seats we are, sure of his client, and within ten minutes the writer is one of the friendliest witnesses the Committee has had the pleasure of. He throws in every name he can think of, including his college roommate, childhood friend."

I said, "No, that won't happen and for more solid reasons than your honor or even mine. I told you I can't make quick changes."

Joe told Pollitt that he thought he understood about no press and the half-empty room: the Committee had kept our appearance as quiet as they could. Joe said, "That means they're frightened of us. I don't know whether that's good or bad, but we want the press here and I don't know how to get them."

He didn't have to know. The room suddenly began to fill up behind me and the press people began to push toward their section and were still piling in when Representative Wood began to pound his gavel. I hadn't seen the Committee come in, don't think I had realized that they were to sit on a raised platform, the government having learned from the stage, or maybe the other way around. I was glad I hadn't seen them come in — they made a gloomy picture. Through the noise of the gavel I heard one of the ladies in the rear cough very loudly. She was to cough all through the hearing. Later I heard one of her friends say loudly, "Irma, take your good cough drops."

The opening questions were standard: what was

my name, where was I born, what was my occupation, what were the titles of my plays. It didn't take long to get to what really interested them: my time in Hollywood, which studios had I worked for, what periods of what years, with some mysterious emphasis on 1937. (My time in Spain, I thought, but I was wrong.)

Had I met a writer called Martin Berkeley? (I had never, still have never, met Martin Berkeley, although Hammett told me later that I had once sat at a lunch table of sixteen or seventeen people with him in the old Metro-Goldwyn-Mayer commissary.) I said I must refuse to answer that question. Mr. Tavenner said he'd like to ask me again whether I had stated I was abroad in the summer of 1937. I said yes, explained that I had been in New York for several weeks before going to Europe, and got myself ready for what I knew was coming: Martin Berkeley, one of the Committee's most lavish witnesses on the subject of Hollywood, was now going to be put to work. Mr. Tavenner read Berkeley's testimony. Perhaps he is worth quoting, the small details are nicely formed, even about his "old friend Hammett," who had no more than a bowing acquaintance with him.

MR. TAVENNER: . . . I would like you to tell the committee when and where the Hollywood section of the Communist Party was first organized.

MR. BERKELEY: Well, sir, by a very strange coincidence the section was organized in my house. . . . In June of

1937, the middle of June, the meeting was held in my house. My house was picked because I had a large living room and ample parking facilities. . . . And it was a pretty good meeting. We were honored by the presence of many functionaries from downtown, and the spirit was swell. . . . Well, in addition to Jerome and the others I have mentioned before, and there is no sense in me going over the list again and again. . . . Also present was Harry Carlisle, who is now in the process of being deported, for which I am very grateful. He was an English subject. After Stanley Lawrence had stolen what funds there were from the party out here, and to make amends had gone to Spain and gotten himself killed, they sent Harry Carlisle here to conduct Marxist classes. . . . Also at the meeting was Donald Ogden Stewart. His name is spelled Donald Ogden S-t-e-w-a-r-t. Dorothy Parker, also a writer. Her husband Allen Campbell, C-a-m-p-b-e-l-l; my old friend Dashiell Hammett, who is now in jail in New York for his activities; that very excellent playwright, Lillian Hellman . . .

And so on.

When this nonsense was finished, Mr. Tavenner asked me if it was true. I said that I wanted to refer to the letter I had sent, I would like the Committee to reconsider my offer in the letter.

MR. TAVENNER: In other words, you are asking the committee not to ask you any questions regarding the participation of other persons in the Communist Party activities?

I said I hadn't said that.

Mr. Wood said that in order to clarify the record Mr. Tavenner should put into the record the correspondence between me and the Committee. Mr. Tavenner did just that, and when he had finished Rauh sprang to his feet, picked up a stack of mimeographed copies of my letter, and handed them out to the press section. I was puzzled by this — I hadn't noticed he had the copies — but I did notice that Rauh was looking happy.

Mr. Tavenner was upset, far more than the printed words of my hearing show. Rauh said that Tavenner himself had put the letters in the record, and thus he thought passing out copies was proper. The polite words of each as they read on the page were not polite as spoken. I am convinced that in this section of the testimony, as in several other sections — certainly in Hammett's later testimony before the Senate Internal Security Subcommittee — either the court stenographer missed some of what was said and filled it in later, or the documents were, in part, edited. Having read many examples of the work of court stenographers, I have never once seen a completely accurate report.

Mr. Wood told Mr. Tavenner that the Committee could not be "placed in the attitude of trading with the witnesses as to what they will testify to" and that thus he thought both letters should be read aloud.

Mr. Tavenner did just this, and there was talk I couldn't hear, a kind of rustle, from the press section. Then Mr. Tavenner asked me if I had attended the meeting described by Berkeley, and one of the hardest

things I ever did in my life was to swallow the words,
"I don't know him, and a little investigation into the
time and place would have proved to you that I could
not have been at the meeting he talks about." Instead,
I said that I must refuse to answer the question. The
"must" in that sentence annoyed Mr. Wood — it was
to annoy him again and again — and he corrected
me: "You might refuse to answer, the question is
asked, do you refuse?"

But Wood's correction of me, the irritation in
his voice, was making me nervous, and I began to
move my right hand as if I had a tic, unexpected, and
couldn't stop it. I told myself that if a word irritated
him, the insults would begin to come very soon. So I
sat up straight, made my left hand hold my right
hand, and hoped it would work. But I felt the sweat
on my face and arms and knew that something was
going to happen to me, something out of control, and
I turned to Joe, remembering the suggested toilet in-
termission. But the clock said we had only been there
sixteen minutes, and if it was going to come, the bad
time, I had better hang on for a while.

Was I a member of the Communist Party, had I
been, what year had I stopped being? How could
I harm such people as Martin Berkeley by admitting I
had known them, and so on. At times I couldn't follow the reasoning, at times I understood full well that
in refusing to answer questions about membership in

the Party I had, of course, trapped myself into a seeming admission that I once had been.

But in the middle of one of the questions about my past, something so remarkable happened that I am to this day convinced that the unknown gentleman who spoke had a great deal to do with the rest of my life. A voice from the press gallery had been for at least three or four minutes louder than the other voices. (By this time, I think, the press had finished reading my letter to the Committee and were discussing it.) The loud voice had been answered by a less loud voice, but no words could be distinguished. Suddenly a clear voice said, "Thank God somebody finally had the guts to do it."

It is never wise to say that something is the best minute of your life, you must be forgetting, but I still think that unknown voice made the words that helped to save me. (I had been sure that not only did the elderly ladies in the room disapprove of me, but the press would be antagonistic.) Wood rapped his gavel and said angrily, "If that occurs again, I will clear the press from these chambers."

"You do that, sir," said the same voice.

Mr. Wood spoke to somebody over his shoulder and the somebody moved around to the press section, but that is all that happened. To this day I don't know the name of the man who spoke, but for months later, almost every day I would say to myself, I wish I could tell him that I had really wanted to say to Mr. Wood: "There is no Communist menace in this country and you know it. You have made cowards into liars, an ugly business, and you made me write a letter in which I acknowledged your power. I should have gone into your Committee room, given my name and address, and walked out." Many people have said they liked what I did, but I don't much, and if I hadn't worried about rats in jail, and such. . . . Ah, the bravery you tell yourself was possible when it's all over, the bravery of the staircase.

In the Committee room I heard Mr. Wood say, "Mr. Walter does not desire to ask the witness any further questions. Is there any reason why this witness should not be excused from further attendance before the Committee?"

Mr. Tavenner said, "No, sir."

My hearing was over an hour and seven minutes after it began. I don't think I understood that it was over, but Joe was whispering so loudly and so happily that I jumped from the noise in my ear.

He said, *"Get up. Get up.* Get out of here immediately. Pollitt will take you. Don't stop for any reason, to answer any questions from anybody. Don't run, but walk as fast as you can and just shake your head and keep moving if anybody comes near you."

I am looking at a recent letter from Daniel Pollitt, who is now a distinguished professor of law at the University of North Carolina. He doesn't comment on the run we made out of the building, the fastest I ever made since I was a child late for class. But he remembers that we went to a restaurant for a Scotch and then another and another and waited for Joe, who never came, and that he wondered how with only a dollar fifty in his pocket he could pay the check. He was saved, he said, by a friend of mine from the State Department who came by and paid the bill. But according to my diary, he has mixed that day with one that occurred a few weeks before. Rauh did join us, kissed me, patted Pollitt on the shoulder a couple of times, ordered us sandwiches and said to me, "Well, we did it."

"What did we do? I don't understand why it was over so fast."

Rauh said he didn't know whether they had made a legal mistake in reading my letter into the record, but for the first time they had been put in a spot they didn't like, maybe didn't want to tangle with. They could call me again, but they'd have to find another reason, and so he hadn't sent me to jail after all, and everything had worked just fine.*

---

* Many people through the years have asked me why the Committee did not prosecute me. I could only repeat what Rauh thought the day of the hearing. On the completion of this book, I phoned him to ask if, after all these years, there could be another explanation. He said, "There were three things they wanted. One, names which you wouldn't give. Two, a smear by accusing you of being a 'Fifth Amendment Communist.' They couldn't do that because in your letter you offered to testify about yourself. And three, a prosecution which they couldn't do because they forced us into taking the Fifth Amendment. They had sense enough to see that they were in a bad spot. We beat them, that's all."

I kept saying, "My, my," through the sandwich, too tired to understand much of what he said. And then we were back in Joe's office and Joe was calling people, and somewhere along the line somebody spoke to Arthur Krock of the *New York Times,* who said he had admired my position and thought we would find the *Times* report sympathetic. As a matter of fact the press was, in general, very good, and five days later in the *Post* Murray Kempton wrote a piece, "Portrait of a Lady," that gave me great pleasure.

I called Hammett and left a message I'd be home for dinner. I didn't want to talk to him. I didn't want to say, even by inference, "See, I was right and you were wrong," because, of course, I had not been right, if by right one means what one wanted to say, didn't say, and the fact that I got off without being prosecuted didn't prove that I had been right.

I took a late afternoon plane to New York. I felt fine until I began to vomit after the takeoff. As I washed my face, I remembered Sophronia, my nurse, saying to the cook or to anybody else who could be trapped into listening about me, "The child's got no stomach. No matter how sick she is with what, she can't throw up. She try, I try, but it ain't to be."

It was to be that night and into the next two days. I remember very little about those days except that I was always thirsty, sleepy, and saying to myself, "From now on, you make no phone calls to anybody. You will wait for them to call you. Life has changed."

Life had changed and there were many people who did not call me. But there were others, a few friends, a few half-strangers, who made a point of asking me for dinner or who sent letters. That was kind, because I knew that some of them were worried about the consequences of seeing me.

But the mishmash of those years, beginning before my congressional debut and for years after, took a heavy penalty. My belief in liberalism was mostly gone. I think I have substituted for it something private called, for want of something that should be more accurate, decency. And yet certain connecting strings have outworn many knives, perhaps because the liberal connections had been there for thirty years and that's a long time. There was nothing strange about my problem, it is native to our time; but it is painful for a nature that can no longer accept liberalism not to be able to accept radicalism. One sits uncomfortably on a too comfortable cushion. Many of us now endlessly jump from one side to another and endlessly fall in space. The American creative world is not only equal but superior in talent to their colleagues in other countries, but they have given no leadership, written no words of new theory in a country that cries out for belief and, because it has none, finds too many people acting in strange and aimless violence.

But there were other penalties in that year of 1952: life was to change sharply in ordinary ways.

We were to have enough money for a few years and then we didn't have any, and that was to last for a while, with occasional windfalls. I saw that coming the day the subpoena was first served. It was obvious, as I have said, the farm had to be sold. I knew I would now be banned from writing movies, that the theatre was as uncertain as it always had been, and I was slow and usually took two years to write a play. Hammett's radio, television and book money was gone forever. I could have broken up the farm in small pieces and made a fortune — I had had an offer that made that possible — and I might have accepted it except for Hammett, who said, "No, I won't have it that way. Let everybody else mess up the land. Why don't you and I leave it alone?", a fine sentiment with which I agree and have forever regretted listening to. More important than the sale of the farm, I knew that a time of my life had ended and the faster I put it away the easier would be an altered way of living, although I think the sale of the farm was the most painful loss of my life. It was, perhaps, more painful to Hammett, although to compare the pains of the loss of beloved land one has worked oneself, a house that fits because you have made it fit thinking you would live in it forever, is a foolish guess-game.

But something so remarkable happened five days before we moved that it turned pain into something else, something almost good, a gift that made me think maybe luck was not gone forever and past punishment might someday be of little importance.

We had always had deer on the farm, and before Westchester County forbade shooting them, Hammett would kill our allotment and we'd have splendid venison through the winter. Every now and then on a winter walk, deep in the woods or on a riding path, I would come almost face to face with a deer, or a doe with fawns. Often on a slight rustle in the distance I would immediately crouch down to wait, sometimes for a long time, and sometimes rewarded by the sight of a deer quite close to me. Deer are the most lovely of all living things to me, and once I found myself in the ridiculous position of standing deep in a snowbank, holding out my arms to a doe and crying in shocked rejection when, startled, she fled at high speed.

Two years before we sold the farm, before there was any trouble, I had extended a large lawn into a narrow lane of fruit trees, meaning to clear an area behind them, fence it in, and have a small deer park of my own. I had planned that I would visit them only on the days when I thought I had worked hard enough, or had, in some way, earned the pleasure of them. But I had done only the work of clearing the woods when the farm had to be sold.

It was bought by a pleasant couple — there had been a number of men with strange proposals of all cash, ready with plans for subdivisions — and the agreement with the buyers was that we were to be out within a month. The hardest of the work was over: the tractors, the boats, the farm implements, the animals had been sold or given away.

Five days before the storage people were to come for the furniture, I was upstairs packing something or other in my bedroom, which was directly above a charming workroom I had long ago made for myself. A large terrace was off the workroom, facing the line of fruit trees and the deer park that was never to come, bordered on one side by a beautiful rock garden planted by a long-dead expert before we bought the house.

Hammett came to the foot of the stairs and in a whisper said, "Come down. Be very quiet. When you get to the last few steps, crouch very low so that you can't be seen through the window." His voice was excited and happy, and as I ran down the steps he was standing far to the side of the large windows. He made a down motion with his hand. I crawled the steps after the landing, crawled across the room, and he raised me slowly to my feet. Before me was the finest sight of my life, so stunning, so unbelievable, that I began making choking sounds until Hammett put his hand over my mouth.

On the wide road from the lake at least twenty deer, moving slowly, were joining a larger group who were wandering up the shorter path through the fruit trees. All of them, small and large, pale and darker, moved without fear, stopping along the way to nibble at the May buds. Eight of them had moved close to the terrace, were looking up at the house, but without curiosity, as if it were another kind of tree. Then a group of them went past the terrace and up into the rock garden, where they found such lovely things to eat that they were joined by six or seven others. In all, the parade from the lake road, the deer that took the fruit path, the deer in the rock garden, certainly numbered forty or fifty does, bucks, fawns, moving as I think few people have ever been allowed to see them, untroubled, not even on their usual alert for smell or rustle. Once, after about an hour, Hammett and I changed positions. Then, a long time later, he crawled across the floor, piled a small chair high with cushions, and pushed it for me to sit on, putting it a proper distance from the windows. I remember looking at my watch: it was a few minutes past four. It was after six o'clock when the deer began to disappear, in small family groups, some heading for the main road and then flying back to the rock garden, some on a new course into a large stand of pines, most of them going as they came, by the road to the lake. There were four last stragglers who stopped to examine a small dogwood immediately off the terrace, but one of our dogs barked in the distant kennels and the deer were off into the woods. Neither Hammett nor I had said a word during the hours of the deer, but I guess I made sounds once in a while, because he would laugh and pat my head.

We ate dinner without speaking. Later that evening I went into his room. He was staring at the wall, two books lying next to him.

"We had something nice. Who managed that?"

He smiled and turned his face away from me.

"Look," I said, "go back to New York. I'd rather do the last few days' packing by myself. It's O.K. now."

He didn't answer me and I went back to packing. A large part of the next morning he stood by the window and then went out into the woods, as he had for so many years, carrying a lunch sandwich in his pocket. That night he said, "Can you handle the movers by yourself?"

"Yes," I said. "We shouldn't say goodbye to this place together. It will make it bad for both of us."

He left the next morning. Kitty, the Bensons and I continued to sort and pack. It was Kitty who reminded me that we hadn't yet touched the attic. I was irritated on climbing the ladder to the attic to find that Hammett had used it for many years to hide the nutty and expensive gadgets that he liked so much and then forgot; there were a hundred feet of telephone wire; a giant unopened package which proved to be a rubber boat; a chess set that had been carefully arranged but never used; a small ice chest that had evidently been tested and was now broken; two suits of horsehide made for hunting on very cold days; a toy train, mysteriously addressed to the son of a friend but never mailed; two expensive casting rods and reels, in addition to the four that were already in use downstairs; a set of Spengler in German, a language Dash couldn't read; two pairs of fur slippers with my name on the package; an unopened extension ladder, and odds and ends of stuff that I couldn't identify. The telephone wire being the most inexplicable of the mess, I mailed it to him in New York, and for at least a year the unopened package sat in a corner and neither of us ever mentioned it.

The furniture movers were to come early on a Monday morning. On Sunday afternoon I had a telephone call from Henry Wallace asking me to come and have a farewell supper with him and Ilo, his wife. I had known Wallace very well, having been one of the people who had backed his third party presidential bid in 1948, contributed to it at a time when I should not have contributed to anything, and traveled with him on speechmaking tours. As the months went on I became more and more convinced that I had made a foolish and thoughtless move. I had seen a third party as necessary in this country — I still do — but I had not wanted all energies turned toward a presidential campaign. I had thought we would concentrate on wards, districts, even neighborhoods, building slow and small for a long future, and I disagreed that so much energy and money, all of it, in fact, was being gambled on a man about whom I had many doubts. My doubts had nothing to do with my fondness for Wallace: his rare, odd pieces of knowledge, often remarkable in their practicality, often wacky in their mysticism, interested me; he was serious about the state of America, open about his fears for the future, but there was no doubt that the powerful hand of Roosevelt had held tight rein over the conflicts in Wallace's nature and the strange digressions of his mind.

By that Sunday of June 1952, the day before I was to move, the Progressive Party had disintegrated. Wallace and I had stayed friends, in part because I had, a few years before, been willing to gamble a fair amount of money on his favorite project, the cross of the Rhode Island Red hen with the Leghorn in an attempt to get a high-laying chicken that was also a good food bird, a cross that, unlike his brilliant experiments with corn, never worked. But long before that Sunday, Wallace had turned bitter about the Progressive Party, telling people that I was the only person connected with it whom he had ever trusted. (I was never sure he said it; it didn't sound like him.)

When Wallace left Washington, and before the formation of the Progressive Party, he had bought a farm less than a half-hour from mine. We saw each other first as neighbors and then, of course, a great deal during the Progressive Party's busy days — never around Hammett, who left the room any time Henry came into it — and then less and less after the

Progressive Party campaign. I was uneasy about the rather strange statements that came from Wallace afterwards: a suspicious innocence of what had been, an unpleasant pouting quality.

During the early autumn of 1948, four or five of us were eating lunch together on the day of a large evening rally. When lunch was finished Wallace suggested that he and I take a walk. (One of us at the lunch, as always, turned back to supplement the waiter's tip: Henry never left more than five percent and there had been certain embarrassing scenes.) When we had walked for a while, he asked me if it was true that many of the people, the important people, in the Progressive Party were Communists. It was such a surprising question that I laughed and said most certainly it was true.

He said, "Then it is true, what they're saying?"

"Yes," I said. "I thought you must have known that. The hard, dirty work in the office is done by them and a good deal of the bad advice you're getting is given by the higher-ups. I don't think they mean any harm; they're stubborn men."

"I see," he said, and that was that.

But several weeks later, in a kind of policy meeting, I saw that he was restive and wary; the Communists in the room, and there were, perhaps, four of them out of the ten people in the meeting, were pushing too hard and with not much sense on an issue the particulars of which I no longer remember, but with which I disagreed. I was now convinced that my constant pleas that we turn attention and money away from the presidential campaign and put them into building small chapters around the country in the hope of a solid, modest future, not into a flashy national campaign which had no hope of working, were defeated forever. I knew I had lost the argument not only with Wallace, who wanted all money and attention for his presidential run, but with the Communist faction, who carried a great deal of weight with the non-Communist group.

That night I called a friend — I did not know if he was a member of the Party or if he was close to them — and asked if he would arrange a meeting for me and whoever he considered the two or three highest-ranking members of the Communist Party.

Two afternoons later we met in my friend's apartment. There were three men there, all high officials because I recognized their names. My friend left us alone and I said that there seemed to me to be six Communists in the Progressive Party, two of them intelligent and flexible, four of them stubborn and unwise, interested in very little except the imposition of their own will.

I said, "I think I understand Henry Wallace. He does not oppose your people because what they want fits at the minute what he wants. But when he loses, he will turn on all of you, and you will deserve it. You have a political party of your own. Why do you want to interfere with another political party? It's plain willful meddling and should stop because it is going to fail. Please think about what I am saying."

I went into another room to get myself a drink and to give them time alone. When I came back, two of the men were gone. The one with the most important title was waiting for me.

He said, "We believe that what you have said makes sense because we know the men you are talking about. But you have the illusion, shared by many people, that the Communist Party is dictated to by a few officials. The truth is that we have no control over the men you think stubborn and willful. We will repeat to them what you have said, and I, for one, will say that I agree with you. But don't count on any change."

I don't know what he ever said or did, but there was no change, and after our failure in the election — failure to make even the number of votes I thought we would get — Wallace withdrew in a strange humor and, not long after, began to declare openly that he had not known about the Communists in the Progressive Party. I, because I had told him, have to believe that he was lying, but there is a chance that so strange a nature had put aside our conversation at a time when it didn't suit him to hear it. He was not a simple man.

On the Sunday night before the Monday I was to leave the farm, I was very tired and not anxious to make the half-hour drive to the Wallace house. But there was something kind about the supper invitation, some wish, I thought, to declare his good will. When I arrived Ilo Wallace made a pleasant picture on the porch. She said Henry was out doing something with the gladiolas, but would be back soon. He was cross-breeding gladiolas, and I remembered Hammett's remark that he'd be better off leaving things alone and cross-breeding himself. Ilo was a pretty woman, grown heavy in middle age, and a rather puzzling lady. She had told me, from time to time, stories of her past. One of them pleased me, although no amount of tactful, and then untactful, questions ever made clear whether she knew the humor of what she said, or was simply recounting something she remembered but which had not disturbed her. She told me that on the day of their marriage Henry's father, who had been Secretary of Agriculture under both Harding and Coolidge, had given them a wedding present of a new Ford. She and Henry came out of the church after the ceremony, and Henry was so pleased with the sight of the Ford that he ignored the kissers and congratulators, went immediately to the car, and drove off. It was thought odd, but people said he was testing it for her comfort until a half-hour passed, and then another. Toward late afternoon he returned, and called out from the driver's seat, "Get in, Ilo, I'd forgotten you."

She did not smile when she told the story, but

she showed no resentment, and I came to think that no deep emotion had ruled, or even entered, her life.

We chatted that Sunday evening about nothing until Henry appeared, and then Ilo said the cook was on holiday, so she, Ilo, would cook our supper.

I wanted a drink badly, but I knew that was out of the question. The talk between Henry and me was weary and worthless, the way it always is between people who would like to say things they have decided not to say. Ilo finally announced supper. The Wallace farm was an egg farm and Ilo's dinner consisted of two poached eggs for Henry put on two shredded wheat biscuits, a horrid sight, made more insulting by one egg on shredded wheat for me and one for Ilo. It was the sight of this stingy, discourteous supper that made me say I had already eaten and didn't wish anything else. I waited until they had finished, it didn't take long for such food, and while Ilo was undisturbed — what could disturb a woman who put eggs on shredded wheat? — obviously Henry had noticed my frowns. When I rose to go, he said he had a present for me. That was such an unusual event that I stood staring out in the darkness while he put something large in the luggage rack of my car. We all shook hands, said we must see each other soon.

Toward noon of the next day, in the middle of watching the movers carry out the furniture, I remembered the gift in the luggage rack. Benson and I opened it and found a fifty-pound bag of manure, a rather impractical gift for a farm that I no longer owned, not too dainty a gift for a woman. I was never to see Wallace again, although I don't think the eggs or the manure had much to do with that.

That Monday was not a happy day. People came to call for the things they had bought — the dairy cows, the ducks, the chickens, the eleven small poodles, the farm machinery, the boats, the fine butchering knives and tables, the four handsome Angus, the canning and sausage-making machinery, the hundreds of items that make a good working farm. I knew that day I would never have any of them again. But whenever I said that to myself I also said that I was lucky ever to have had them at all, and that is what I feel today, these many years later. Loss of money can take away what you like and have been good at, but in my case, I am now certain that without the trouble I would have stayed in one place, one frame too long. I am angry that corrupt and unjust men made me sell the only place that was ever right for me, but that doesn't have much to do with anything anymore, because there have been other places and they do fine. If I had stayed on the farm I would have grown old faster in its service. There are not many places or periods or scenes that you can think back upon with no rip in the pleasure. The people who worked for us must feel the same way, because each Christmas we still send each other gifts, but we do not meet because all of us fear, I think, the sad talk of a good past. Benson, my farmer, is dead, but his wife lived to raise a good son, and whenever I talk to her I remember the picture of her fat, cheerful little boy sitting on the terrace steps with Hammett, a bitter ex-Catholic, who was taking the boy through his catechism and explaining with sympathy the meaning of the ceremony.

Notes from a diary of May 10, 1952. I called Marc Blitzstein and we met at the Russian Tea Room. I told him about my appearance before the Committee in a week or ten days and asked him not to tell anybody. I was telling him because it meant that I couldn't do the narration for *Regina* * at the concert on June 1. I should have told him before, but even though I love Marc, and we have been close friends, there are times I don't like to listen to him. I expected a lecture, I didn't know what kind, but a lecture, so I started off by saying Lennie would do as well, maybe better. Blitzstein stared at me for a while, then he said, "No. We can't call you off, and you can't call yourself off. We'd all look like cowards." I said maybe I was, I couldn't stand the idea of being hissed

* *Regina* is the opera Blitzstein wrote based on my play *The Little Foxes.*

by an audience, and that was what would happen. He
said, "I don't think they will hiss you, and if they do,
I won't have it. I'll just come out and say I don't want
my music played before such people, and we'll give
them their money back and send them home."

I laughed because I could hear him doing it, en-
joying it. When we left each other he said, "You've
got bigger things to worry about. Forget the concert,
we'll face it the night it happens."

From a diary of June 2. So there I was last night
in my Committee-Balmain dress. Marc got to the Y
before I did, both of us early. He says the lobby is
already full, the house will be sold out, do I know if
they allow standing room. I said I didn't know anything, just fear. He said to shut up, but he is frightened, too, because he moves around so much backstage and nods at me every time he passes me. I
stand in the wings. The grips are fanning themselves
because it is a hot night, but I am cold. I am in much
worse shape than the day I came before the Committee, maybe because this is my racket and audiences
have always frightened me. A voice says, "Need a
drink?" I turn to see a large Irishman with red hair.
I said I sure did, but I had forgotten to bring anything. He takes his right hand from behind his back
and hands me the largest shot of bourbon I've ever
seen. I get it down too fast and he brings me a stool
and a glass of water. Then he disappears. Marc
passes again, goes down into the pit with the musi-

cians. But the liquor makes things worse. Now I am really shaking, and in moving around on the stool I rip my stocking on the wood rungs. The young red-head reappears and says I am on the wrong side of the stage for my entrance. We cross and I stumble over a cable.

He says, "You need another drink. One is bad for the stomach."

When we get on the other side, the redhead takes his place at the lighting board, calls out something to somebody, and in a few minutes another hand gives me another bourbon. I hesitate and the redhead says: "Best thing going." I drink half of it. I see the curtain go up and remember that I am the first person on the stage. I can't get off the stool. The redhead says, "Go on. Go on fast."

I turned, I guess in full sight of the right-hand side of the audience, and said, "I wouldn't say it if I wasn't drunk, but if you're not married I hope you will consider me."

He laughs and says, "Get onstage."

I got halfway across the stage, staring straight ahead, saying something to myself, some prayer, I don't remember. Suddenly there is thunderous applause. It is so unexpected that I stop dead center in such shocked surprise that the first few rows began to laugh. Then the audience rose, applauding, and I face it, unable to move. For a second I think that the applause is meant for the musicians, but they have

risen too, and Marc tells me later that I looked behind me to see if the applause was meant for somebody else. Then I hear Marc's voice from somewhere
saying, "For Christ's sake, move to your stool." I
want very much to cry, but I moved to the stool,
opened the pages of my narrative, and couldn't believe the calm sounds that were coming out of me
about *Foxes* and what Marc had done with it in
Regina. I usually read too fast, but this time it is
just right, slow and even. At the end of one section of
my narrative the singing began — I haven't even seen
the singers come onstage — and when nobody is looking at me anymore, I reach into my pocket for a
handkerchief. I haven't any. Somebody makes a sound
to my right and I see that the redhead has crossed
backstage and is beckoning to me from the wings,
very close to me. I get off my stool. I shouldn't move,
of course, but he seems to me now the best friend
I've ever had and I wouldn't think of disobeying him.
He hands me a half-bottle of ginger ale and a paper
cup. He says, "It's bourbon. Carry it back with you."

I HAVE NO OTHER NOTES for that night. We got
through it fine, everybody says, and it was a great
success. Two days later I try to find the redhead's

name, but nobody seems to know. I call the stage-
hands' union, describe him, and they say they'll find
out who was working that night. But I never heard
from them, and I've never seen the redhead since.

F OR ALMOST A YEAR after my hearing before the
Committee and after the sale of the farm, I have very
little memory and only occasional diary notes. Hammett, disliking New York, had rented a small house
from friends in Katonah and made it smaller and
more miserable with the gadgets from Pleasantville
and the enormous amount of books that finally were
so piled on chairs and the floor that one moved around
the room like a snake and found only a small corner
of a couch to sit on.

I had two polyp operations on my throat that
year, and I think I remember the operations because
they came two days after the opening night of the
revival of *The Children's Hour*. I had directed the
revival, and my memory of the operations is lying in
bed thinking about my place in the theatre. Kermit
Bloomgarden, the producer, had given a pleasant
opening night party in a small Italian restaurant and,
toward midnight, our press agent phoned in the *New
York Times* review. I stood outside the phone booth

as Kermit repeated the review to me, thinking what a fool I was to be so nervous about what anybody said about a play written eighteen years before. The theatre is, by necessity, often a silly business, and that night I seemed to me the sucker of the world.

And during that year I had what could be called, by romantic courtesy, an affair with a man I had turned down when I was twenty-one years old. His bastard nature, when I was young, seemed comic; but when I was in my forties it seemed plain cruelty in space, inflicted for the pleasure of the pain he caused anybody who came near him. I was fair game that year and he admitted that he had first telephoned me thinking just that, to pay me back for a twenty-five-year-old "insult." He did pay me back, but not for long, and when he found out it was not for long he followed me to Rome, put himself in a hospital, and announced that the doctor said he had cancer. Would I cable his children? His children did not come, but each day when I went reluctantly to call on him we had a farewell scene of a different variety: one day he would be cheerful about the full life he had lived, the pleasure his enemies would have on the news of his death. (He said I needn't deny that and I didn't.) Another day, in the middle of my visit, his eyes closed in what he said were racking pains that made death desirable. On two visits he discussed with me the disposition of property he didn't own: all was to go to me, he said, because his children had not re-

sponded to the cable. He left me a Picasso he had
never owned and twelve Regency chairs that were in
storage but he couldn't remember the name of the
storage company. I did not enjoy these visits, but I
cannot deny that no matter what I knew about him, I
was touched by his bravery. Toward the end of the
week I bumped into his doctor in the hall. The doctor
was an American, so it was not language that made us
not understand each other until I mentioned his
patient's terrible cancer pains, was there nothing to
be done? The doctor said his patient had a mild
attack of colitis, he never had any need to be in a
hospital, and they were putting him out that day. I
went back, stuck my head in the patient's door, said
all that, and he screamed, "The doctor is a liar. He
told me I had cancer." I have never seen the non-
cancer non-invalid since, although about eight years
ago he sent me a paper parasol from Japan.

I believe that for years I have remembered this
unimportant affair — far too big a term for what
happened between us — because, punished by what
I thought was a group of political villains, I was
evidently driven to find another kind of villain and
another kind of punishment. Whatever I think comic
now, I did not find comic the night I stood on a dock
in Palm Beach and, from a distance, watched him em-
brace a woman. When he saw me on the dock, he
came toward me, smiling. He said, "That was my
sister-in-law. My disgusting brother has left her again

without a cent." It seemed more than silly to tell him
that he had no brother and so I took myself back to
New York to think that trouble makes trouble, and
that is what is most to be feared about it. I was learning that change, loss, an altered life, is only a danger
when you become devoted to disaster.

Money was beginning to go and go fast. I had
gone from earning a hundred and forty thousand a
year (before the movie blacklist) to fifty and then
twenty and then ten, almost all of which was taken
from me by the Internal Revenue Department, which
had come forward with its claim on the sale of a play
that the previous administration had seemingly agreed
to. I didn't understand it then and I don't now; my
lawyer advised a compromise. But the compromise
allowed was small, and the collection very large.

The loss of money made less difference than I
thought; middle-class security is a faith from which I
have never recovered, but that has certain virtues.
Chiefly, I was bored by the necessity of counting what
could be had for dinner, what couldn't, how much
housework I could do by myself, how many dresses I
wanted that I couldn't have, the miserable amount that
Hammett, despite my protests, would take from the
safe each month, living on far too little, never buying
anything for himself anymore except food and rent.
That made me sad: never in the ten years since the
Internal Revenue cut off his income — two days after
he went to jail — did he ever buy a suit or even a tie,

until the week of the opening night of *Toys in the Attic,* when he bought new dinner clothes and, I believe, had a happy evening at the play and the nice feel of a new suit. In 1960 *Toys in the Attic* was a great success and, in the money sense, the bad times were over. Hammett died a year later, but at least that year was lived in security.

I was in rome on Mrs. Shipley's temporary passport in 1953. I was working on a movie for Korda, to be directed by Max Ophuls, and had chosen to live in Rome because it was cheaper than any other place. I had a small apartment with a kitchenette in a tacky hotel in the vulgar Parioli section of the city. I had a few friends, but it was a period of not wanting to see people, wanting only to save money, doling it out on kitchenette food, walks instead of taxis, and disliking all that so much that I would go on aimless spending sprees. The spending sprees became so obsessive, so ridiculous that I finally figured out a way to deal with them: for that year and for years after, wherever I was, I gave myself the equivalent of five dollars a week to throw away. It was spent almost always in the equivalent of a ten-cent store on junk I didn't need: games, bad candy, nasty-colored lipsticks, toys that

fell apart, paper books I had already read, small sewing boxes and sewing gadgets because I was teaching
myself to mend and repair. My five-dollar day was
always on a Monday, and it turned out I had found a
good solution: once the nonsense stuff was bought, I
felt better and wasn't tempted by the clothes or shoes
or bags that were very pretty that year in Rome.

I was more alone than I had ever been before,
but life was pleasant and I saw much of the hidden
treasures of the city because I was looking for cheap
restaurants or markets and thus came across many
beautiful small churches and interesting buildings in
sections of the city I would ordinarily have missed.

Once in a while I saw a few friends or Americans who were passing through, and sometimes I
would be summoned to Korda's yacht, usually off
Antibes, for a script conference or a reading of what
I had written. He and Ophuls were pleased with what
I had done and I would return to Rome and plug
away at the adaptation of a Nancy Mitford novel that
I would never have touched in the good days, hoping
that I wouldn't always have to earn a living doing
what I didn't like.

I have few sharp memories of those many months
in Rome, except for the drama that was to happen in
July. Mrs. Luce was our ambassador at the time, and
that was not well considered by anybody I knew
except a couple I had met years before in New York.
The wife had been a radical and I had seen her

around and about, and the husband, I was told, was a
writer. They were friends of Mrs. Luce, often dinner
guests, and that puzzled many people: why Mrs. Luce
would like people with radical histories. Since I have
no final proof that they were involved in what happened to me, I have here changed their names to Dick
and Betty. I do have proof, however, that although he
was a stringer for a newspaper service, he was also
working for the CIA and, jack-of-all-trades, for the
Vatican.

It has little to do with their place in my life that
one night I bumped into Sam and Frances Goldwyn,
and as we sat in an outdoor café we were greeted by
Dick and Betty, who had with them two almost naked
starlets and a man with his shirt opened to his navel
and bracelets to bind both arms below the elbow. I
don't think Goldwyn had ever seen a man with so
much open flesh and jewelry, so his attention had
wandered by the time Betty said that her friend Mrs.
Luce had been affected by a mysterious poison, perhaps from falling bits of plaster from the ceiling.
Goldwyn heard the word poison in his own fashion —
which was not unusual — and asked how persons
could fall from the ceiling, what were they doing
there? And maybe he was close to the truth: Mrs.
Luce did, in time, go home because she was officially
ill, although many Italians believed she had been recalled for meddling too openly in their government.

But that was not yet July. One morning of that

month I woke up to read in the *Rome Daily American*
that Senator McCarthy had subpoenaed me. (He had
not subpoenaed me, but I took the newspaper headline to mean that it would be served on me in Rome
when he found that I was not in New York.) My
limited passport had only ten days to go and I had,
up to that day, taken for granted that Mrs. Shipley
would extend it for another period. But I knew that
with the news of McCarthy, and no passport, Korda
would not, could not go on employing me.

I started out for the cable office, deciding that I
would send McCarthy my Rome address, but a few
cups of coffee later I knew there was something the
matter with that kind of showing-off because most
certainly he knew that I was in Rome and where to
reach me. When I realized that it had taken me an
hour to figure that out, I knew that I had better not
rely on my own judgments. I telephoned the office of
Ercole Graziadei, a fine lawyer whom I'd met several
times, a man who had a splendid reputation as an
anti-Fascist under Mussolini. He said that although I
could not be sure of the newspaper story, it was now
certain the American consul in Rome would not issue
an extension of my passport. He also said that he
believed Rome was not a good place for me because
the Italian government often took their orders from
Mrs. Luce and they could pick me up or harass me on
an even lesser charge than evading a subpoena, or for
using a passport that had expired. I said I thought

I'd go back to New York immediately. He laughed
and said he thought that was foolish: I would be
giving up a job I needed, walking into trouble. Why
didn't I go up to London for a few days, where the
government didn't take orders from Washington,
and try for an extension of my passport there? That
seemed good sense and would give me a chance to
phone Hammett from an untapped instrument and
find out about the McCarthy story. Graziadei said his
son-in-law would buy me an afternoon ticket to London. I was to go back to my apartment and do
exactly whatever I did every day at that hour, take no
baggage except what I could put in a shopping bag
or purse, take a taxi to the Excelsior Hotel, spend ten
minutes in the bar, take another taxi from the Excelsior to the airport, where his son-in-law would be
waiting for me.

I did exactly what Graziadei told me. I left my
hotel at two-fifteen, took a taxi to the Excelsior, bought
myself a stiff drink, took another taxi to the airport.
The airport was empty at that hour except for the
son-in-law, who was waiting for me with my ticket. I
was reading a magazine when the loudspeaker called
my name, saying there was a telephone call for me. I
did not move until the loudspeaker came again and
then I thought I had to answer the phone because
the girl at the desk who had checked me in could see
me from where she was making the announcement.
When I got to the desk the girl said, "The secretary

of the Contessa ———— wishes to speak with you."
I had met the elderly Contessa several times, had
once been to her palazzo for lunch, and once had
tea with her as she explained for what seemed like
many hours her English background and the pains
of being married to an Italian. Before I picked up
the phone, of course I asked myself how her secretary
could know I was at the airport. A woman spoke into
the phone in so English an accent that I began to
think it was too English. She said she was the Contessa's secretary, could I come to a small dinner
party at the end of the week when the Contessa returned to Rome? I repeated the invitation, stalling
for time and then I said yes, I would be glad to come
and I was at the airport to meet an American friend.
I telephoned Graziadei, who said he didn't believe it
was the Contessa, that he thought somebody had tried
to follow me to the airport, lost me, and was now
making sure. In any case, it was too late to worry and
to send news from London.

It was such a nervous ride to London that I was
there before I realized that I must find a hotel, certainly something cheap. But on the way to a taxi I
told myself that I was going back to Claridge's, like
the old days. I would be less nervous there and to hell
with money for a few days.

I did, indeed, feel nice in the pretty room and
was extravagant enough to order a good dinner, and
to be very glad to see the old valet I had known for

years, who said he'd be happy to wash my messy cotton dress and deliver it by eight in the morning.

At ten the next morning I was sitting on a bench in the American consul's outside office. When the lady at the desk examined my passport she said it would be necessary for me to see the consul. An hour or two later she told me he was busy and perhaps it would be better if I came back at three in the afternoon. It was obvious now that things weren't going to be easy. I took a sandwich to the National Gallery, exactly the way I had done two or three times a week during the war when Myra Hess would give lunchtime concerts. I had returned looking for the music that was no longer there, no longer needed for anybody except maybe me. I sat wondering why driving into V-2 bombs every morning as we shot a documentary on the London docks in 1944 had worried me less than my present disorder.

When I returned to the consulate, the clerk at the desk took me immediately into the consul's office. He was a pleasant, good-mannered man, and when we had finished chatting about his mother having been born in New Orleans, wasn't that a coincidence, he said that he could not renew or extend my passport, the request would have to go back to Washington and he would have to wait for an answer. I should have known that, but I heard myself say, "I can't stay here long, it's expensive and I have only one dress and it's raining." He was too good-mannered, I guess, to ask why I had come to London without a second dress. He said he would call me as soon as he heard from Washington.

I said, "Would it be possible for you to cable that unless I can have the extension this week I will lose my job?"

He smiled and said perhaps it would be best if I sent that message in another cable to Mrs. Shipley.

I didn't send it. I walked back in the rain, wondering where I could find a cheap dress and raincoat, decided not to bother, and ended up in bed.

Toward evening I remembered the pub at the next corner where I had gone so many times during the war, and afterwards, and where the charming fat lady who ran it had always been kind and friendly. She and her middle-aged son, Oliver, were glad to see me. She had a shrewd eye because when she sat down with our beers she asked me if I was feeling sick. I said no, just troubled. We talked for a long time, she told me she was getting married again and moving to Devon, and she shouted to Oliver, who brought me a large piece of cold roast beef. I guess I had had too many beers, too much of something, because there could have been no reason to cut my right hand with the knife unless I had tried to do it. I don't know to this day if I said that out loud or if I only thought that bad luck had been sitting near that hand for a long time, and if I couldn't break the luck I would join that large army of people who know that no matter what they do it will turn out wrong, and they end up doing nothing, or doing what they shouldn't do. I know only that Oliver was over-disturbed by my cut, cleaned it, and his mother asked why I was out in such weather without a raincoat and went to get a poncho she said a customer had left behind months before and I should keep it. I never saw either of them again, although we exchanged many postcards and I had an announcement of Oliver's wedding to somebody called Poly. The pub closed down a few years later. In 1970 I had a letter from Oliver that says, "I think you want to know that Ma died ten months ago. The man would not marry, so she managed another pub and died easy in bed with my uncle not her brother, my dead father's brother. My Poly is no way sorry to see Ma go but I was and wants to thank you for wedding present."

Two days went by after my night in the pub. I couldn't make myself call anybody I knew in London. I don't any longer know what I did with those days except once I took a boat ride up the river. On the third morning a girl called from the consulate and asked me to come over at eleven. I was there at ten, for no purpose, I thought, except to make myself more nervous. At eleven o'clock I was told that the consul was in a meeting and would I come back at two. I wanted to say, "Tell him to go to hell," but I didn't, and regretted the days when I would have. But at two the consul was pleasant about the rain stopping, he liked London but the traffic was getting very naughty, and Mrs. Shipley had extended my passport for another three months.

I phoned Hammett from the London airport and made a date with him to go to a number we had long ago arranged if either one of us might be in trouble and didn't want to be phone-tapped. Then I called Graziadei with the good news and he said that was fine, there were no further Rome newspaper accounts of my subpoena, but it might be wise to stay in London. I said I couldn't do that, my dress was dirty, and he laughed and said women were women.

When I arrived back in Rome there was no mail of any importance and the clerk said nobody had asked for me. I telephoned the Contessa. Her secretary, who did not have an English accent, said the Contessa had been away from Rome for the last few weeks and would not be returning for a month.

Then I went down to the Grand Hotel and put in a call to Dash at the arranged number and time. He said there had been nothing in the New York newspapers about a subpoena for me. I said that even though I now had an extended passport, maybe I should come home and tell McCarthy I was ready when he was ready, but before I finished that sentence Dash said, "Stop the honor child stuff and stay where you are. McCarthy's going bats. Let him go bats without your help." Then I told him about the call from the Contessa at the airport and there was such a long pause that I said, "Hello, are you there?" and he said yes, I was to give him a minute to think, he wasn't a machine. I said the call at the airport had frightened me and he said that was good because it should have.

Then he said, "What's a big tip in a Wop hotel?"

"Two or three dollars."

"O.K. Give the top bellboys five dollars each. Give the same to each telephone operator. Give the desk clerks ten dollars and tell them there's ten dollars more for anybody who can tell you who followed you, or asked for you at the desk, or showed any interest the day you went to London. Then don't get your usual impatient. Let all that sink in for a few days and maybe it will turn up something and maybe it won't."

I said I thought he was awfully smart and he said, "Lilly, please stop admiring me for nothing."

The next morning I distributed the money and asked the questions. Nobody knew anything, everybody looked puzzled, everybody took the money. Two days later — I went for a walk every day around four o'clock — a middle-aged man whom I recognized as a kind of part-time relief bellboy was standing outside my grocery store as I walked down the block. He made some kind of motion to the man who owned the shop and the owner made a motion through the window for me to come inside. The store was empty, but

we went into the back room and the bellboy began to
talk. I could understand almost nothing of what he
said, and the owner, who spoke English, said not to
pay any attention, his cousin didn't talk well, something had always been the matter with him, but not too
much. He said his cousin had come to him the night
before to say that I was wasting my money on the
tips because the hotel people were frightened to talk.
He had told his cousin not to be frightened, that I
would certainly pay him for what he could tell me,
and would not say a word that could bring him into
"the affair." I said I would certainly pay him and not
bring him into "the affair," that I was in no position
to make trouble and didn't want any for myself. Then
the translation began and its first interruption was
surprising: the owner said his cousin wanted to know
if I had ever acted in the movies or was an anarchist.
I said I wrote movies, didn't agree with anarchists.
That was not well received because the bellboy refused to speak for a while, chewing on a thumbnail.
The grocery man got impatient and pushed his cousin's hand away from his mouth. The translation for
the next five minutes — it wasn't easy because the
bellboy would wander off the subject and the transla-
tor would bark at him — boiled down to one of the
desk clerks being a police agent, and two of the telephone operators, and it was not the first time that the
man had come to ask about my movements, with
whom I had gone out, what visitors, and from time

to time been handed my mail. The bellboy said that one of the clerks had seen him listening, hanging around, and had told him that if he ever opened his mouth about "the gentleman" he would be deported. The store owner had evidently never heard this part before, because he grew angry and shouted that Fascism was over, and what the hell was the matter with his cousin for not telling him about the deportation shit before? He himself would go and denounce the clerk, he wanted no Fascist in his family.

There was nothing I could do but wait out the tirade. When the owner went to serve a customer I tried my bad Italian: what was the name of the man who had inquired for me so often? He did not know the name. What did he look like? He was American, past thirty, tallish, blond, always clean, losing some of his hair. When the owner came back I asked him to ask his cousin if the man's accent was like mine. No. I imitated a Westerner. No. I tried something vaguely Southern. Yes, that was nearer. Did the man give money to the clerks or phone operators? The bellboy didn't think so, the man was "official" and he thought they got their money by the month, that it came through an office. What kind of "official" did he think the man was? The grocer laughed; didn't I know that the Americans, my people, had many agencies, and all of them paid for information? After that practice had been denounced for too many minutes I gave the grocer what amounted to twenty

147

dollars, he divided it with his cousin, and I said there would be ten more if he could call me when the man came again, or if he could find out the man's name. We all shook hands, clucked over the state of the world, and I walked for two hours trying to place the description of my caller. It fitted too many people.

But the following morning I found a note under my door. It said, in printed English letters, "The man's name is Dick ———. Put ten dollars American in envelope and leave envelope at grocery store." It was signed Sophia Sanitation, an interesting name. I did exactly that, the grocery store owner took it, nodded, and went back to work. There is a possibility that Sophia Sanitation worked in the hotel; it is more probable that the bellboy and the store owner knew the man's name the day before and saw another ten dollars in the delay.

But now I thought it best to leave Rome. I was never to hear from McCarthy or anything further about a subpoena, but Dick and Betty have frequently, in unimportant ways, crossed my life. The lady was to have an affair with a friend of mine many years later and to tell my friend that one of the reasons she wanted to leave her husband was the shame she felt about his CIA connections. When the love affair was over she went back to her husband. He evidently had a fit of nerves over the indiscretion of his wife and wrote the ex-lover that, indeed, he had once been

CIA, was no longer, but that his wife was still a valuable and highly paid agent and he hoped that would remain a secret with my friend. It didn't.

I have no idea why the CIA was interested in me in Rome, but I've always believed that Dick gave the subpoena story to the Rome newspapers with an aimless hope that he'd turn up something, have a little news to send his bosses that week. In those days, unlike these days when the level of interference is higher and more dangerous, the' CIA was picking up all kinds of clowns on a piecework basis, and when you work that way the more casseroles you cook up the greater the chance one of them will taste good enough to pay off.

But nothing much was to go right that year. Korda, who had liked my script, did not like it when it was finished and refused to pay me what was due. He forgot to tell me that he couldn't pay me, that it had nothing to do with the virtues or faults of the script; he had gone bankrupt a week before.

And so I came back to New York and did nothing for a while. Then, not unexpected, we had no money left. I took a half-day job in a large department store, under another name, arranged by an old friend who worked there. I was in the grocery department and that was not unpleasant, but I kept it a secret because I knew it would worry Hammett. About six months later, an aunt I liked very much died in New Orleans, and left me a larger sum than I ever thought she could have saved in her hardworking life.

I guess I began to write again, although I can't remember what, maybe because it was just practice stuff.

Hammett and I rented a house that summer on Martha's Vineyard and the fine black lady, Helen, came back to work because now we could afford to pay her again. Nothing was as it had been, but because it had been bad, small things seemed better than ever — the occasional rental of a catboat for a day's sail, a canoe for the pond, a secondhand car, grocery bills I didn't have to worry so much about. We had a good summer.

And it was the summer of the Army-McCarthy hearings. For us, of course, they came too late to make much difference and seemed a wild mess. The boozy, hospital-patched face of McCarthy, sometimes teasing and gay as in the good days, often caught in disbelief that he was where he was, and angry. He and his boys, Roy Cohn and David Schine — the brash but less assured older brothers of Haldeman and Ehrlichman — were, indeed, a threesome: Schine's little-boy college face, Cohn plump of body, pout of sensual mouth, and McCarthy, a group breaking up before our eyes after years of a wild ride. Bonnie, Bonnie and Clyde, shooting at anything that came to hand on the King's horses that rode to battle in official bulletproof armor.

Then Mr. Stevens of the Army, a strangely unsympathetic figure, and the lawyer Joseph Welch, certainly a Boston gentleman, remembered for that highly admired sentence, "Have you no sense of decency, sir?" I thought the sentence funny; had it really taken Welch so long to find that out, or was it a good actor's instinct for proper timing?

Because, of course, McCarthy was finished long before the hearings began. It wasn't because he had become too daring and taken to fooling around the sacred precincts of the Army, it was simply and plainly that most of America was sick of him and his two kiddies.

The editor and critic Philip Rahv, an early anti-Communist and then an early anti-anti-Communist, had said it a year before in one of his least decipherable growls: "Nothing can last in America more than ten years. McCarthy will soon be finished." And that, I think, was the truth, just that and not much more. We were not shocked at the damage McCarthy had done, or the ruin he brought on many people. Nor had we been surprised or angered by Cohn and Schine playing with the law as if it were a batch of fudge they enjoyed after the pleasure of their nightly pillow fight. We were bored with them. That and nothing more.

There were many broken lives along the path the boys had bulldozed, but not so many that people needed to feel guilty if they turned their backs fast enough and told each other, as we were to do again after Watergate, that American justice will always prevail no matter how careless it seems to critical outsiders.

It is not true that when the bell tolls it tolls for thee: if it were true we could not have elected, so few years later, Richard Nixon, a man who had been closely allied with McCarthy. It was no accident that Mr. Nixon brought with him a group of high-powered operators who made Cohn and Schine look like cute little rascals from grammar school. The names and faces had been changed; the stakes were higher, because the prize was the White House. And one year after a presidential scandal of a magnitude still unknown, we have almost forgotten them, too. We are a people who do not want to keep much of the past in our heads. It is considered unhealthy in America to remember mistakes, neurotic to think about them, psychotic to dwell upon them.

N OTHING MORE WAS TO HAPPEN to me. I began to write plays again and in 1958 to get movie offers that I no longer wanted; the taste had gone.

It is true, as I have said, that Hammett was never again allowed to have a nickel of his own money and that the emphysema which had started in the Aleutians was to end in cancer of the lungs. Those last years were not good for him, but he managed them fairly well, with no complaints about what had been done to him, even refusing to call the police on two occasions when people, or official people, fired shots through the window of his cottage. But none of those years were as bad as they could have been and were for many people.

I recovered, maybe even more than that, in the sense of work and money. But I have to end this book almost as I began it: I have only in part recovered from the shock that came, as I guess most shocks do, from an unexamined belief that sprang from my own nature, time, and place. I had believed in intellectuals, whether they were my teachers or my friends or strangers whose books I had read. This is inexplicable to a younger generation, who look upon the 1930's radical and the 1930's Red-baiter with equal amusement. I don't much enjoy their amusement, but they have some right to it. As I now have some right to disappointment in what the good children of the Sixties have come to.

Maybe what I still feel is best summed up in an evening I once spent in London with Richard Crossman, then an editor of the *New Statesman and Nation* and a member of Parliament. It was about a month after Hammett had gone to jail and Crossman knew nothing of my connection to Hammett. He had turned

to me, as the only American in the room, to say that
it was a disgrace that not one intellectual had come
to Hammett's aid, that if such a case had happened
in London he, and many others like him, would have
protested immediately on the grounds that it is your
right to believe, my obligation to stand by even in
disagreement. I remember that Kingsley Martin, the
intelligent, cranky editor of the *New Statesman and
Nation*, very worried, was trying to tell Crossman of
my relation to Hammett. He ignored Kingsley to say
that it took an Englishman a long time to fight for a
liberty but once he had it nobody could take it away,
but that we in America fought fast for liberty and
could be deprived of it in an hour.

In every civilized country people have always
come forward to defend those in political trouble.
(There was once even some honor in being a political
prisoner.) And there were a few here who did just
that, but not many, and when one reads them now the
words seem slightly timid, or at best too reasonable.

And it is now sad to read the anti-Communist
writers and intellectuals of those times. But sad is a
fake word for me to be using; I am still angry that
their reason for disagreeing with McCarthy was too
often his crude methods — the standards of the board
of governors of a country club. Such people would
have a right to say that I, and many like me, took too
long to see what was going on in the Soviet Union.
But whatever our mistakes, I do not believe we did our

country any harm. And I think they did. They went to too many respectable conferences that turned out not to be under respectable auspices, contributed to and published too many CIA magazines. The step from such capers was straight into the Vietnam War and the days of Nixon. Many of the anti-Communists were, of course, honest men. But none of them, as far as I know, has stepped forward to admit a mistake. It is not necessary in this country; they too know that we are a people who do not remember much.

I HAVE WRITTEN HERE that I have recovered. I mean it only in a worldly sense because I do not believe in recovery. The past, with its pleasures, its rewards, its foolishness, its punishments, is there for each of us forever, and it should be.

As I finish writing about this unpleasant part of my life, I tell myself that was then, and there is now, and the years between then and now, and the then and now are one.